W9-BWZ-124

# BIBLE TRUTH
# FOR SCHOOL SUBJECTS

Volume II

# LANGUAGE ARTS/ENGLISH

**READING
WRITING
LITERATURE
SPEECH
LISTENING
FOREIGN LANGUAGES**

## Ruth C. Haycock, Ed.D.

**Association of Christian Schools International**
**P. O. Box 4097, Whittier, CA   90607**

Scripture quotations not indicated otherwise are from the King James Version of the Bible.

Quotations designated NASB are from the New American Standard Bible, © The Lockman Foundation 1960, 1962, 1963, 1968, 1971, 1972, 1973, 1975.

# Table of Contents

# Foreword

As this book is read and studied, it becomes evident that many years of research and thought preceded the writing. It is clear that the Word of God is preeminent in each chapter. Dr. Ruth Haycock, respected Christian school educator and student of the Book, has done more than write a book. She has shared part of her life work in the philosophy of Christian education.

The style of the book is easy to follow. The concepts at the start of each chapter are lucid and valid. The Scriptures are natural, not forced. The projects are thoughtful, worth the effort. The book is balanced with strength in each section.

An unusual feature of Ruth Haycock's writing is this: the book has value for every teacher of whatever grade level or subject area. Those who teach language arts will benefit especially. All will benefit because every teacher uses language arts in teaching. Teachers in training, young teachers, and veteran teachers will find instruction here that they have never heard before.

I believe that a good book is intellectually challenging and upbuilding to the soul -- a mental and a spiritual exercise. This is such a book. It causes my heart to say with deepening conviction, "Thank you, Lord, for your remarkable gift of the language arts."

Roy W. Lowrie, Jr., President
Association of Christian Schools International
Newtown Square, Pennsylvania

# Preface

The purpose of this handbook for teachers is to provide Scriptural concepts related to the various subjects within the language arts, English and foreign language areas. God has much to say that is relevant, and we must find it and teach it!

My own concern for teaching from a Biblical vantage point spans many years, and includes input from Mark Fakkema's and Frank Gaebelein's books, John Blanchard's classes on the Christian school, the contrasts I saw between Bible college teaching and secular graduate study, teachers in workshops and Christian school conventions, the constant struggle to organize college courses in education that are Biblical.

The opportunity to participate in the National Institute of Christian School Administration came to me, and with it the additional challenge to study the Word in depth as it relates to school subjects and educational philosophy. I increasingly found that each workshop allowed time for only an introduction to the integration of Biblical truth with school subjects. Out of that realization came the sense of urgency to make something available to teachers which could be a companion to lesson plan books and teacher's manuals.

Many who teach in our Christian schools do not have extensive Bible training. Others have studied God's Word as it relates to sin, salvation, God, man and other theological topics, but not as it relates to the subjects commonly taught in elementary and secondary schools.

As I searched the Scriptures in preparing this volume, I have been constantly amazed at all that God says about the language arts areas. He obviously cares about our use of language for His glory, whether it be the ability to produce and take advantage of that which is written, or to use oral language to accomplish His purposes. My expectation was that this volume would be considerably shorter than Volume 1 on Social Studies, but instead, it is longer! I didn't know the Lord cared so much!

In spite of its length, this compilation is incomplete. It will serve its purpose however, if it stimulates teachers to study the Scriptures to see what God has to say, and then to use what they find in their classrooms.

Many people have contributed to this book by their encouragement and interest. Special thanks is due James Braley and others of the Association of Christian Schools International for their willingness to cooperate in this project. The many hours of typesetting and paste-up have been done by Doris Manuel and Mary Thompson, dear friends whose personal hours have been filled because of their concern for this kind of ministry.

Tentative plans are for Volume 3 to include science and mathematics, and Volume 4 other major school subjects. We shall appreciate your interest and prayers in these big projects. Your suggestions concerning helpful resources are most welcome.

Ruth C. Haycock
1701 Aberdeen Terrace
Winston-Salem, N.C. 27103

# Introduction

It has often been said, *The Christian pupil attending a secular school is being sheltered from the truth: consequently he is conforming to the world rather than to the image of Christ.* In a general way those of us involved in Christian schools are quick to agree, recognizing that without the written Word of God and the living Word, Jesus Christ, a child is being cheated. He is not getting the things in life which are most crucial to his becoming what God intends.

Even in a Christian school however, it is very possible that a child may also be sheltered from truth, especially in his academic studies. He may be involved in Bible class and chapel, be subject to Christian standards and discipline, be active in Christian service, and still be getting primarily a secular academic education. What he is taught, and how he is taught, may be so similar to what is done in the neighboring non-Christian school that a visitor would not detect a difference.

As Christian schools have multiplied, many devoted Bible-believing teachers have moved from public to Christian schools. They have rejoiced in the freedom to mention the Lord and all that is most precious to them. They have been happy for higher standards of discipline and achievement. In many cases though, they have brought to their new schools the old viewpoint of their subjects. It is what they know best. They learned it in the public schools themselves. They built upon that foundation in college. They learned how to teach it and then for some years used the secular humanistic textbooks and teacher's manuals which were provided.

New teachers too have often had all their training either in secular institutions or in Christian colleges where their academic and education professors were the pro-ducts of humanistic colleges and graduate schools. Too frequently the feeling is, "After all, reading is reading, language arts is language arts, isn't it, regardless of where you teach it? Why then expect it to be different in a Christian school?"

If we actually believe that the Bible is authoritative in every area in which it speaks, in history and science as well as in salvation and prayer, we are obligated to find out what it says about every topic we teach. If we fail to present what God says but teach other aspects of a subject, we shelter pupils from the truth and give them only part of the story.

What we do teach may be purely humanistic and opposed to the truth found in the Bible, or it may be true as far as it goes, but incomplete. In either case pupil thinking is being shaped according to the world's pattern. God asks instead for transformed lives, not conformed to the world, but based on renewed minds able to prove *what is that good and acceptable and perfect will of God.*

If Christian schools are to be Christian in the academic areas and to present a Biblical life and world view, teachers must become increasingly familiar with what the Word says in each area; they need to search for ways to involve pupils in learning, ways which enable them to understand and accept that Biblical viewpoint which is part of God's perfect will. In addition, Christian teachers must assist one another in producing textbooks and other materials which are based on Biblical principles.

It is not enough that we moralize in Bible classes to teach socially acceptable or even Christian conduct. Neither is it adequate that we use incidents from history, or observations from science, to illustrate spiritual truth. Though history and science furnish many possible object

lessons, their use in this fashion is not true integration of truth from Scripture and truth from other sources. It is not equivalent to searching out what God actually teaches about reading, or foreign language, or our use of speech, and then teaching what we find as part of the academic discipline.

Again, neither does the use of sentences from the Bible in a grammar lesson, or Scriptural words in a spelling lesson, necessarily mean that a Biblical view of a subject is taught. So also, the frequent quotation of Bible verses in workbooks or textbooks, or the use of Biblical themes for art work, does not guarantee that the subject itself is being taught Biblically. While education in a Christian school should surely include a study of Bible sentences and words, and the use of Biblical quotations and themes, the integration of truth is more and deeper.

Basic to the whole concept of teaching God's truth in every area, and of helping pupils to see all truth as from God, are two prerequisites for the Christian school. **First**, the Bible must be thoroughly taught at each grade level as the inerrant Word of God, whether it deals with trusting Christ or the qualification for leadership, with prayer or history. **Second**, Christian aspects of a subject must be included as part of that academic discipline, not relegated to Bible class alone.

For example, as the literary classics are studied, Christian writings must be included; as the Middle East is considered historically or geographically, Palestine and Israel must be given a rightful place. To fail here is to say to young people that Bible and the academic subjects are separate - that only in Bible class do we consider what God says. With such a message conveyed to them, students will graduate with what Rushdoony calls "intellectual schizophrenia" and defeat the whole purpose of the Christian school.

The Bible gives much attention to communication. Not only is it concerned with God's communication to man, but also with our interpersonal communication. God might have created and never told us about His creation. He might also have loved us without telling us so, but love that is not communicated is cold and unrecognized.

Human interaction too depends on the language arts, and God is careful to show how crucial our use of reading and writing, speaking and listening is to our social relationships. God cares what we say and how we say it.

In the humanistic society around us language and literature are major tools for changing and thinking of youth. Constant exposure to that which is crude or sadistic, licentious or unpatriotic is a method designed to break down earlier moral teaching. A comparison of recent dictionaries with Noah Webster's 1828 edition shows alarming changes in the meanings of words. If Christian schools are to fulfil their purposes in developing mature believers, they must give attention to a Biblical view in the language-related subjects.

In each of the chapters a list of Biblical concepts will be presented first. Then will follow Scripture passages which may be used in the classroom as a basis for study and investigation.

Rousas J. Rushdoony, *Intellectual Schizophrenia* (Philadelphia: Presbyterian and Reformed Publishing Co., 1961).

---

## Christian Maturity

Christian maturity means having a total Christian world view, with Christian convictions on every conceivable subject. To get acquainted with Jesus Christ as personal Saviour is only the beginning of a life of growth and development. Christianity extends into the intellectual arena of life, and Biblical principles relate to all areas, including government, education, business, economics, ecology, law, medicine, etc. Personal piety is good and pleasing to God, but that form of "pietism" which restricts Christianity to the personal dimensions of life is inadequate. The Bible tells us to "do good to all men" (Gal. 6:10), and there is no way to accomplish this without relating Christian truths and principles to all areas of life.

Quoted from **Responsible Citizens Newsletter, August 1978** in *Christian Focus* (Lubbock, TX), author unknown.

# 1

## Language Arts / English in General

## CONCEPT SUMMARY

1. God is a communicating God; He wants us to know His thoughts.

2. God communicated with man throughout history: with individuals in relation to His will for them, and with messengers who were to convey His message to others.

3. God speaks to man through His creation.

4. God speaks by the actions which He performs.

5. God gave His message in written form, the Bible.

6. God's greatest message is His Son's coming to earth to live a perfect life, die for our sins, and rise again.

7. We are responsible for knowing and heeding what God says.

8. The ability to communicate with one another and with God is part of His plan for our lives.

9. We must evaluate the truth of all other communication by the Bible, since it alone is absolute truth.

10. God is concerned that communication be clear and easily understood.

## SCRIPTURAL BACKGROUND

### 1. God is a communicating God; He wants us to know His thoughts.

Amos 4:13

*The Lord is creator and controller of the earth, the One who declareth unto man what is his thought."*

Jeremiah 44:2-4

*2   Thus saith the Lord . . . 4   . . . I sent unto you all my servants the prophets rising early and sending them saying, Oh, do not the abominable thing that I hate.*

Hebrews 1:1, 2

*1   God who at sundry times and in diverse manners spake in time past unto the fathers by the prophets, hath in these last days spoken unto us by his Son . . . .*

Also Isaiah 42:9; 45:18, 19; 48:15, 16.
Revelation 1:1-3, 19; ch. 2, 3; 22:10.

### 2. God communicated with man throughout history.

### a. God spoke to individuals in relation to His will for them.

Genesis 1:28-30

*28   And God blessed them [Adam and Eve] and God said unto them, Be fruitful, and multiply . . . 29   And God said, Behold I have given you every herb . . . it shall be for meat . . . .*

2:16, 17

*16   And the Lord God commanded the man, saying, Of every tree . . . eat: 17   But of the tree of the knowledge of good and evil . . . not eat . . . .*

3:8-19

*8   And they heard the voice of the Lord God walking in the garden . . . 9   And the Lord God called unto*

*Adam, and said unto him, Where art thou? 10   And he said, I heard thy voice . . . .*

4:9-15

*9   And the Lord said unto Cain, Where is Abel thy brother? And he said,  I know not . . . .*

6:13-22; 7:1-4; 8:15-17; 9:1-17

God speaks to Noah.

PROJECT: In the Book of Acts find incidents when God communicated directly with Paul.

## b. God spoke with prophets who were to convey God's message to others.

Exodus 3:4 through 4:23

God's conversation with Moses out of the burning bush.

4:27

God speaks to Aaron.

Isaiah 1:2, 18, 20

Isaiah speaking: *2 Hear, O heavens, and give ear, O earth: for the Lord hath spoken . . . 18 Come now, let us reason together, saith the Lord . . . 20 . . . for the mouth of the Lord hath spoken it.*

Jeremiah 1:1-6

*1 The words of Jeremiah . . . 2 To whom the word of the Lord came in the days of Josiah . . . 4 Then the word of the Lord came unto me, saying, 5 . . . I ordained thee a prophet . . . 6 Then said I, Ah, Lord God! behold I cannot speak; for I am a child . . . .*

25:3, 4

Jeremiah speaking: *3 From the thirteenth year . . . even unto this day [i.e., in the twenty-third year]. . . .*

*the word of the Lord hath come unto me and I have spoken unto you . . . 4 And the Lord hath sent unto you all his servants the prophets, rising early and sending them; but ye have not hearkened . . . .*

Ezekiel 1:3

*The word of the Lord came expressly unto Ezekiel . . .*

1:28 - 2:7

*28 . . . This was the appearance of the likeness of the glory of the Lord. And . . . I heard a voice of one that spake. 1 And he said unto me, Son of Man, . . . I will speak unto thee. 2 . . . I heard him that spake unto me. 3. And he said unto me, Son of man, I will send thee . . . 7 And thou shalt speak my words unto them . . . .*

Revelation 1:1

*The Revelation of Jesus Christ, which God gave unto him to shew unto his servants things which must shortly come to pass; and he sent and signified it by his angel unto His servant John.*

## 3. God speaks to man through His creation.

Job 12:7-10

Beasts, fowls, fish and the earth itself point to the fact of God.

Psalm 19:1-6

*1 The heavens declare the glory of God; and the firmament showeth his handywork.*

97:6

*The heavens declare his righteousness, and all the people see his glory.*

Matthew 6:26-32

God's care of birds, flowers and grass tells of His care for us.

Romans 1:18-20

*18 For the wrath of God is revealed . . . 19 Because that which may be known of God is manifest in them; for God hath shewed it unto them. 20 For the invisible things of him from the creation of the world are clearly seen, being understood by the things that are made, even his eternal power and godhead; so that they are without excuse.*

## 4. God speaks by the actions which He performs - by the things He does to show truth.

Exodus 7:3, 5

*3 And I will harden Pharaoh's heart, and multiply my signs and wonders in the land of Egypt . . . 5 And the Egyptians shall know that I am the Lord, when I stretch forth mine hand . . .*

9:14

After six plagues: *14 For I will at this time send all my plagues upon thine heart, and upon thy servants, and*

*upon thy people; that thou mayest know that there is none like me in all the earth.*

11:7

God explaining about the coming death angel. *7 But against any of the children of Israel shall not a dog move his tongue, against man or beast: that ye may know how that the Lord doth put a difference between the Egyptians and Israel.*

**12:24-27, 42**

God commanded the regular observance of the Passover because He wanted His work communicated to the next generation. Also 13:8-10, 14-16.

**19:4**

God expected His people to learn something from observing His activities. Also 20:18.

**Isaiah 41:17-20**

Here speaking of a time yet future: *When the poor and needy seek water, . . . I the Lord will hear them, I the God of Israel will not forsake them: 18 I will open rivers . . . I will make the wilderness* (desert) *a pool of water . . . 19 I will plant . . . 20 That they may see, and know, and consider, and understand together that the hand of the Lord hath done this, and the Holy One of Israel hath created it.*

**45:3**

God speaking to Cyrus who was yet future: *3 And I will give thee the treasures of darkness, and hidden riches of secret places, that thou mayest know that I, the Lord, which call thee by thy name, am the God of Israel.*

**49:22, 23, 26**

God promises judgment to Israel's enemies, with the result that they will know that He is the Lord. *22 Thus saith the Lord God, Behold, I will lift up mine hand to the Gentiles, and set up my standard to the people . . . 23 And kings . . . shall bow down to thee with their face toward the earth, and lick up the dust of thy feet; and thou shalt know that I am the Lord . . . 26 And I will feed them that oppress thee with their own flesh . . . and all flesh shall know that I the Lord am thy Saviour and thy Redeemer, the mighty One of Jacob.*

**Ezekiel 6:7**

God describes His judgment of Israel for idol worship and ends with this statement: *7 And the slain shall fall in the midst of you, and ye shall know that I am the Lord.*

PROJECT: This expression, *ye shall know that I am the Lord,* is found many times in Ezekiel's writings. Look for it and record what He would do that they would know this.

PROJECT: Ezekiel is not the only writer of the Scriptures who records God saying that He would do something so people would know some truth. Watch for similar statements as you read. For example, trace them through Exodus.

**Hebrews 2:3, 4**

*3 How shall we escape, if we neglect so great salvation; which at the first began to be spoken by the Lord, and was confirmed unto us by them that heard him; 4 God also bearing them witness, both with signs and wonders and with diverse miracles, and gifts of the Holy Ghost, according to his own will?*

## 5. God communicated by giving His Word in written form, the Bible.

**2 Timothy 3:16**

*All scripture is given by inspiration of God, and is profitable for doctrine, for reproof, for correction, for instruction in righteousness.*

**2 Peter 1:20, 21**

*20 . . . no prophecy of Scripture is of any private interpretation* [or origination]. *21 For the prophecy came not in old time by the will of man, but holy men of God spake as they were moved by the Holy Ghost.*

**Revelation 22:18, 19**

*18 For I testify unto every man that heareth the words of the prophecy of this book, If any man shall add unto these things, God shall add unto him the plagues that are written in this book: 19 And if any man shall take away from the words of the book of this prophecy, God shall take away his part out of the book of life, and out of the holy city, and from the things which are written in this book.*

6.  **God's greatest message is His Son's coming to earth to live a perfect life, die for our sins, and then rise again.**

Hebrews 1:1-3

*1 God . . . 2 Hath in these last days spoken unto us by His Son, whom he hath appointed heir of all things, by whom also he made the worlds; 3 Who being the brightness of his glory and the express image of his person, and upholding all things by the word of his power, when he had by himself purged our sins, sat down on the right hand of the Majesty on high.*

John 1:14,18

*14 And the Word was made flesh and dwelt among us, (and we beheld his glory, the glory as of the only begotten of the Father,) full of grace and truth. 18 No man hath seen God at any time; the only begotten Son, which is in the bosom of the Father, he hath declared him.*

7.  **We are responsible for knowing and heeding what God says; His Word is authoritative.**

Psalm 119:89

*Forever, O Lord, thy word is settled in heaven.*

119:130

*The entrance of thy words giveth light; it giveth understanding unto the simple.*

119:140

*Thy word is very pure . . . .*

119:151

*. . . all thy commandments are truth.*

119:160

*Thy word is true from the beginning: and every one of thy righteous judgments endureth forever.*

John 8:31,32

*31 Then said Jesus to those Jews which believed on him, If ye continue in my word, then are ye my disciples indeed; 32 And ye shall know the truth, and the truth shall make you free.*

Deuteronomy 27, 28

Here God expresses the curses and the blessings which would come upon Israel for their response to His commandments. Israel is not the church, but the principle of obedience to the Word is the same.

8.  **The ability to communicate with one another and with God is part of God's plan for our lives.**

Genesis 2:20-24

God made Eve - someone on the human level who could communicate with Adam. *"God said, It is not good that the man should be alone; I will make him an help meet for him"* (v. 18).

Exodus 4:10-12

*10 And Moses said unto the Lord, O my Lord, I am not eloquent . . . but I am slow of speech and of a slow tongue. 11 And the Lord said unto him, Who hath made man's mouth? or who maketh the dumb, or deaf, or the seeing, or the blind? have not I the Lord? 12 Now therefore go, and I will be with thy mouth, and teach thee what thou shalt say.*

Jeremiah 1:4-9

*4 The word of the Lord came unto me [Jeremiah], saying, 5 Before I formed thee in the belly I knew thee; and before thou camest forth out of the womb I sancti-fied thee, and I ordained thee a prophet unto the nations. 6 Then said I, Ah, Lord God! Behold, I cannot speak: for I am a child. 7 But the Lord said unto me, Say not, I am a child: for thou shalt go to all that I shall send thee, and whatsoever I command thee thou shalt speak. 8 Be not afraid of their faces: for I am with thee to deliver thee, saith the Lord. 9 Then the Lord put forth his hand and touched my mouth. And the Lord said unto me, Behold I have put my words in thy mouth.*

Galatians 4:6

*And because ye are sons, God hath sent forth the Spirit of his Son into your hearts, crying, Abba, Father.*

I John 1:3

*Truly our fellowship is with the Father, and with his Son Jesus Christ.*

INSTANCES of man and God communicating with one another - a few examples:

Enoch, Genesis 5:22, 24

Noah, Genesis 6:9, 13-22; 7:1-5; 8:15-17; 9:1-17

Abraham, Hagar, Isaac, Moses, Joshua, Gideon, Solomon, Paul (especially see Acts 9:4-6), Ananias (Acts 10:1-19)

PROJECT: Use a concordance or a topical Bible to find passages which speak of communion or fellowship of believers with one another. Communication is basic to fellowship.

## 9. We must evaluate the truth of all other communication by the Bible, since it alone is absolute truth.

Deuteronomy 18:9-14

God told Israel when they entered the land: *13 Thou shalt be perfect with the Lord thy God. 14 For these nations, which thou shalt possess, hearkened unto observers of times, and unto diviners: but as for thee, the Lord thy God hath not suffered thee so to do.*

In other words, though other nations might accept guidance from other sources, God's people were to be distinct in their view of truth.

Isaiah 8:20

*To the law and to the testimony: if they speak not according to this word, it is because there is no light in them.* (Spoken of the sayings of spirits and mediums, but with wider application).

2 Corinthians 6:1-7

*1 We then, as workers together with him, beseech you also that ye receive not the grace of God in vain . . . . 3 Giving no offence in anything . . . 4 But in all things approving ourselves as the ministers of God . . . 7 By the word of truth.*

One criterion for approval of one who ministers is adherence to the Word of God. Therefore what we write or speak must meet this test.

2 Timothy 3:16, 17

*16 All scripture is given by inspiration of God, and is profitable for doctrine, for reproof, for correction, for instruction in righteousness: 17 That the man of God may be perfect, throughly furnished unto all good works.*

## 10. God is concerned that communication be clear and easily understood.

Deuteronomy 27:2-8 (NASB)

God records the fact that just before Israel crossed the Jordan River to enter Canaan, Moses charged the people thus:

*2 . . . you shall set up for yourself large stones 3 . . . and write on them all the words of this law . . . 4 . . . when you cross the Jordan, you shall set up on Mount Ebal, these stones . . . 8 And you shall write on the stones all the words of this law very distinctly* [very plainly in KJV].

Nehemiah 8:8

God describes the reading of the Word by Ezra and his companions in this way: *8 So they read in the book of the law of God distinctly, and gave the sense, and caused them to understand the reading.* Also verses 7, 12, *they understood.*

Ecclesiastes 12:9-11 (NASB)

The record of the way in which Solomon wrote: *9 In addition to being a wise man, the Preacher also taught the people knowledge; and he pondered, searched out, and arranged many proverbs. 10 The Preacher sought to find delightful words and to write words of truth correctly. 11 The words of wise men are like goads, and masters of these collections are like well-driven nails; they are given by one Shepherd.*

Habakkuk 2:2

*And the Lord answered me, and said, Write the vision, and make it plain upon tables, that he may run that readeth it.* [NASB margin: *that the one may read it fluently who is to proclaim it* ].

Matthew 24:15

Christ urged that whoever reads the prophecies of Daniel the prophet: *whoso readeth, let him understand.*

I Corinthians 15:15, 16, 19

Paul is concerned that he both speak and sing with understanding so people may join with him and learn: *15 . . . I will pray with the spirit and with the understanding also: I will sing with the spirit and I will sing with the understanding also. 16 Else ... how shall ... the unlearned say Amen at thy giving of thanks, seeing he understandeth not what thou sayest? 19 ... I had rather speak five words with my understanding, that by my voice I might teach others also* than ten thousand words in an unknown tongue.

GENERAL PRINCIPLE: 1 Corinthians 14:33, 40

*33 For God is not the author of confusion, but of peace.... 40 Let all things be done decently and in order.*

## THE INFLUENCE OF THE BIBLE ON OUR EVERYDAY SPEECH
## SHOWN BY A FEW SAMPLES

The sweat of your brow-Gen. 3:19
My brother's keeper-Gen. 4:9
Fire and brimstone-Gen. 19:24; Rev. 21:8

The fat of the land-Gen. 45:18
Milk and honey-Ex. 3:8
Love thy neighbor-Lev. 19:18

Sabbatical year-Lev. 25:4
Not by bread alone-Deut. 8:3; Matt. 4:4
The apple of his eye-Deut. 32:10

Shibboleth-Judges 12:6
Arose as one man-Judges 20:8
A man after his own heart-1 Sam. 13:14

Set your house in order-2 Kings 20:1
Ears tingle-2 Kings 21:12
The root of the matter-Job 19:28

The ends of the earth-Job 38:13
Out of the mouths of babes-Psalm 8:2
My cup runneth over-Psalm 23:5

At their wit's end-Psalm 107:27
Pride goeth before a fall-Prov. 16:18
Heap coals of fire-Prov. 25:22

Nothing new under the sun-Ecc. 1:9
A little bird told me-Ecc. 10:20
Cast thy bread upon the waters-Ecc. 11:1

Let us reason together-Isa. 1:18
As white as snow-Isa. 1:18
Swords into ploughshares-Isa. 2:4

See eye to eye-Isa. 52:8
The handwriting on the wall-Dan. 5:5, 24-28
Salt of the earth-Matt. 5:13

Turn the other cheek-Matt. 5:39
Go the second mile-Matt. 5:41
No man can serve two masters-Matt. 6:24

Seek and ye shall find-Matt. 7:7
The dead bury their dead-Matt. 8:22
A house divided-Matt. 12:25

The signs of the times-Matt. 16:3
A den of thieves-Matt. 21:13
Washed his hands of it-Matt. 27:24

Physician, heal thyself-Luke 4:23
The laborer is worthy of his hire-Luke 10:7
The truth shall make you free-John 8:32

No respecter of persons-Acts 10:34
The quick and the dead-Acts 10:42
Turn the world upside down-Acts 17:6

A law unto themselves-Rom. 2:14
The wages of sin-Rom. 6:23
All things to all men-1 Cor. 9:22

In the twinkling of an eye-1 Cor. 15:52
Death, why is thy sting?-1 Cor. 15:55
A thorn in the flesh-2 Cor. 12:7

Tossed to and fro-Eph. 4:14
A labor of love-1 Thess. 1:3
Filthy lucre-1 Tim. 3:3

Old wives' tales-1 Tim. 4:7
The root of all evil-1 Tim. 6:10
All of one mind-1 Peter 3:8

The Alpha and Omega-Rev. 1:8
Streets paved with gold-Rev. 21:21
Clear as crystal-Rev. 22:1

- Adapted from a listing published by the Religious Instruction Association, formerly of Fort Wayne, IN.

# 2

## Reading

## CONCEPT SUMMARY

1.  It is God's plan that people should be able to read well.
    a.  God saw to it that His message was written, so people could read it and know for sure what He said.
    b.  God gave commands for people to read the Word.

2.  Christ expected people to read and understand the Scriptures.

3.  Reading is of special importance to those who believe and trust God.

4.  Reading of the Bible is important to growth in knowledge and understanding of life, and our responsibilities in it. The results of such reading can be obtained in no other way.

5.  Reading (or hearing) God's Word requires obedience; therefore our attitude toward it must be distinctive.

6.  To be effective, reading must include understanding.

7.  Public reading, especially of the Word of God, is a sound teaching method. God's Word is effective!

8.  Public reading must be done well to be effective.

9.  Excessive devotion to books is futile as well as tiresome. We can't know it all; we must be selective in what we read.

---

## SCRIPTURAL BACKGROUND

1. **It is God's plan that people should be able to read well.**

   a. **God saw to it that His message was written, so people could read it and know for sure what He said.**

2 Timothy 3:16, 17

*16 All scripture is given by inspiration of God, and is profitable for doctrine, for reproof, for correction, for instruction in righteousness: 17 That the man of God may be perfect, throughly furnished unto all good works.* The word translated <u>scripture</u> literally means <u>writing</u>.

2 Peter 1:20, 21

*20 . . . No prophecy of the scripture is of any private interpretation* (literally, <u>origination</u>). *21 For the prophecy came not in old time by the will of man: but holy men of God spake as they were moved by the Holy Ghost.*

Exodus 31:18; 32:16; 34:1.

God himself wrote the Law, even a second time, after the breaking of the tablets.

17:14

God commanded Moses to write.

Deuteronomy 6:9; 11:20

God commanded parents to write the Law on the door-posts and gates.

Jeremiah 36:2, 3, 23, 28-32

God commanded Jeremiah to write, and then to rewrite what was destroyed. It was crucial to have the Word available to be read.

I John 5:13

*These things have I written unto you that believe on the name of the Son of God; that ye may know that ye have eternal life . . . .* Assurance depends on believing the written Word.

Revelation 1:11, 19 and chapters 2, 3

God commanded John to write what he saw.

**"We must contemplate the import of ignoring the printed word. If you cannot read, you can do only what you are told."**

**-Joseph P. Bean**

## b. God gave commands for people to read His Word.
## Some examples:

Deuteronomy 17:18-20

God commanded long before Israel had a king that, when that time did come, he was to write a copy of the Law.

*19 And it shall be with him, and he shall read therein all the days of his life: that he may learn to fear the Lord his God, to keep all the words of this law and these statutes, to do them: 20 That his heart be not lifted up above his brethren, and that he turn not aside from the commandment to the right hand, or to the left: to the end that he may prolong his days in his kingdom, he, and his children, in the midst of Israel.*

Joshua 1:8

God's command to Joshua: *This book of the law shall not depart out of thy mouth; but thou shalt meditate therein day and night, that thou mayest observe to do according to all that is written therein: for then thou shalt make thy way prosperous, and then thou shalt have good success.*

Isaiah 34:16

As the Lord through Isaiah prophesied of judgment to the nations, He also gave a command to them that they should read His Word and verify the message: *16 Seek ye out of the book of the Lord, and read: no one of these shall fail, none shall want her mate* (referring to the statements in v. 14, 15.)*: for my mouth it hath commanded, and his spirit it hath gathered them.*

Colossians 4:16

The various epistles to the churches were to be read not only by the churches to which they were sent, but by others as well. *16 And when this epistle is read among you, cause that it be read also in the church of the Laodiceans; and ye likewise read the epistle from Laodicea.*

I Thessalonians 5:27

*I charge you by the Lord that this epistle be read unto all the holy brethren.*

I Timothy 4:13

Paul exhorted young Pastor Timothy: *Till I come, give attendance to reading, to exhortation, to doctrine.*

Revelation 1:3

*Blessed is he that readeth, and they that hear the words of this prophecy, and keep those things which are written therein: for the time is at hand.*

## 2. Christ expected people to read and understand the Scriptures.

Again and again He asked, "Have ye not read?" A few examples:

Matthew 12:3-8

When the Pharisees criticized His use of the Sabbath: *3 But he said unto the, Have ye not read what David did, when he was an hungred . . . 5 Or have ye not read in the law, how that on the sabbath days the priests in the temple profane the sabbath, and are blameless? . . . 7 But if ye had known what this meaneth . . . .*

19:3-6

When the Pharisees questioned about divorce: *4 . . . Have ye not read . . . ?*

Also 21:16, 42; 22:31; Mark 12:10, 26.

Mark 10:3

In answer to the question of the Pharisees: *3 And he answered and said unto them, what did Moses command you?*

10:19

To the rich young ruler: *19 Thou knowest the commandments, Do not commit adultery, Do not kill . . . .*

11:17

Casting out the moneychangers: *17 And he taught, saying unto them, Is it not written, My house shall be called of all nations the house of prayer? . . .*

12:24

Answering the Sadducees: *24 And Jesus answering said unto them, Do ye not therefore err, because ye know not the scriptures, neither the power of God?*

PROJECT: Go through the Gospels to find out how many times and in how many ways Christ expressed His expectation that those who questioned Him would have read and studied the Old Testament.

## 3. Reading is of special importance to those who believe and trust God.

Deuteronomy 17:18-20

The future king of Israel was commanded to write a copy of the Law and read and heed it day by day.

Joshua 1:7, 8

When God commissioned Joshua to take the leadership of Israel, He made promises of blessing through Joshua, but He also gave very specific commands to him to read and meditate on what Moses had commanded - i.e., on the book of the Law.

Psalm 1:1-3

God promises fruitfulness and prosperity to one who delights in the law of God and meditates upon it. Reading it is implied.

*1 Blessed is the man . . . 2 . . . his delight is in the law of the Lord; and in his law doth he meditate day and night. 3 And he shall be like a tree planted by the rivers of water, that bringeth forth his fruit in his season; his leaf also shall not wither; and whatsoever he doeth shall prosper.*

Acts 15:19-31

The writing and reading of letters has been an important means of communication among churches, enabling them to learn from one another and fellowship together. After the discussion concerning the need of circumcision for Gentile Christians, it was decided by the church to write to the Antioch church. Their letter brought rejoicing in Antioch (v. 20, 23, 31). Also 1 Cor. 16:2, 3: Rev. 1:11.

1 Timothy 4:13; 2 Timothy 4:13

Those who are preaching and teaching the Word need to read. *13 . . . give attendance to reading . . . 15 Meditate upon these things . . . 13 The cloke that I left at Troas with Carpus, when thou comest, bring with thee, and the books, but especially the parchments.*

All of God's Word is written and therefore to be read and studied.

## 4. Reading of the Bible is important to growth in knowledge and understanding of life and our responsibilities in it; the results of such reading can be obtained in no other way.

Deuteronomy 17:19, 20

It is by reading the Bible that we *learn to fear the Lord . . . to keep all the words of this law and these statutes*, to turn not aside to the right or the left, to continue to be used by the Lord.

Psalm 19:7, 8

Reading of the Word brings conversion of the soul, wisdom to the simple, rejoicing of heart, enlightenment.

119:27

Reading of the Bible results in willingness to talk of God's wondrous works.

119:42

It is by the reading of God's Word that we develop ability to answer those who reproach us.

119:92-95

Delight in what God says results in the ability to stand up even in affliction. *92 Unless thy law had been my delights, I should then have perished in mine affliction. . . . 95 The wicked have waited for me to destroy me: but I will consider thy testimonies.*

119:99, 100

Those who read what God says, meditate upon those truths, and keep God's precepts can have more understanding than professional teachers without the Word. *99 I have more understanding than all my teachers: for*

*thy testimonies are my meditation. 100 I understand more than the ancients, because I keep thy precepts.*

119:104

Through the understanding which results from reading God's Word comes genuineness and honesty. *104 Through thy precepts I get understanding: therefore I hate every false way.* Also v. 133.

119:130

*The entrance of thy words giveth light; it giveth understanding unto the simple.*

119:165

Reading and delighting in the truths of the Bible result in peace of heart in the midst of a troubled world. *165 Great peace have they which love thy law; and nothing shall offend them.* See also Psalm 1:1, 2; 2 Timothy 1:7.

Proverbs 22:20, 21

Reading of the Word provides answers for those who ask us. *20 Have not I written to thee excellent things in counsels and knowledge, 21 That I might make thee know the certainty of the words of truth; that thou mightest answer the words of truth to them that send unto thee?*

1 Peter 2:2

Only by study of the Word do new believers grow. *2 As newborn babes, desire the sincere milk of the word, that ye may grow thereby.*

PROJECT: The Bible is full of statements showing the power of the written Word - many more than are given here. As a long range project, help your pupils to find such statements; or in the study of a specific book of the Bible, keep watch for evidences of the significance of the Word in the lives of those who meditate upon it.

PROJECT: Look especially for statements which liken the Word to some object. Have pupils prepare a chart. Make three columns headed: BIBLE REFERENCE, OBJECT, MEANING OR RESULT. For example: Jeremiah 23:29, Hammer, Breaks down the hardness of heart of those who do not speak the truth (from the context).

## 5. Reading (or hearing) God's Word requires obedience.

### Statements

Deuteronomy 28:1, 2, 15

Moses to Israel: *1 And it shall come to pass, if thou shalt hearken diligently unto the voice of the Lord thy God, to observe and to do all his commandments which I command thee this day, that the Lord thy God will set thee on high above all nations of the earth: 2 And all these blessings shall come on thee, and overtake thee, if thou shalt hearken unto the voice of the Lord thy God. 15 But it shall come to pass, if thou wilt not hearken unto the voice of the Lord thy God, to observe to do all his commandments and his statutes . . . that all these curses shall come upon thee and overtake thee.*

1 Samuel 15:22, 23

Samuel to King Saul: *22 And Samuel said, Hath the Lord as great delight in burnt offerings and sacrifices, as in obeying the voice of the Lord? Behold, to obey is better than sacrifice, and to hearken than the fat of rams. 23 For rebellion is as the sin of witchcraft, and stubbornness is as iniquity and idolatry. Because thou hast rejected the word of the Lord, he hath also rejected thee from being king.*

James 1:22-25

*22 But be ye doers of the word, and not hearers only, deceiving your own selves. 23 For if any be a hearer of the word, and not a doer, he is like unto a man beholding his natural face in a glass: 24 For he beholdeth himself, and goeth his way, and straightway forgetteth what manner of man he was. 25 But whoso looketh into the perfect law of liberty, and continueth therein, he being not a forgetful hearer, but a doer of the word, this man shall be blessed in his deed.* See also Isaiah 48:18.

Matthew 7:24

*Whosoever heareth . . . and doeth . . . I will liken to a wise man, which built his house upon a rock.*

### Examples

Exodus 24:3, 4, 7, 12

*3 And Moses . . . told the people all the words of the Lord, and all the judgments: and all the people an-swered with one voice, and said, All the words which the Lord hath said will we do. 4 And Moses wrote all the words of the Lord . . . 7 And he took the book of the covenant, and read in the audience of the people: and they said, All that the Lord hath said will we do, and be obedient . . . 12 And the Lord said unto Moses, Come up to me into the mount, and be there: and I will give thee tables of stone, and a law, and commandments which I have written; that thou mayest teach them.*

2 Kings 22:8-20; 23:1-25

A wonderful account of what happens when people hear the reading of the Word, see their sin, and repent and make things right - the revival in Josiah's reign.

Nehemiah 8:14-18

After the return from Babylon: *14 And they found written in the law which the Lord had commanded by Moses that the children of Israel should dwell in booths in the feast of the seventh month . . . 16 So the people went forth and brought them, and made themselves booths, every one upon the roof of his house . . . .*

Acts 2:14-41

On the Day of Pentecost: *14 But Peter . . . said unto them . . . 16 . . . This is that which was spoken by the prophet Joel . . . .32 This Jesus hath God raised up, whereof we all are witnesses . . . 36 Therefore let all the house of Israel know . . . that God hath made that same Jesus . . . both Lord and Christ. 37 Now when they heard this they were pricked in their heart, and said . . . what shall we do? 38 Then Peter said unto them, Repent, and be baptized . . . 41 Then they that gladly received his word were baptized . . . about three thousand souls.*

**"To read without reflecting is like eating without digesting."**

**Edmund Burke**

## 6. To be effective, reading must include understanding.

Psalm 119:27

The Psalmist implies that only when we understand God's precepts can we talk of them to others appreciatively. He prays for understanding: *27 Make me to understand the way of thy precepts: so shall I talk of thy wondrous works.*

119:73, 125

*73 . . . give me understanding, that I may learn thy commandments. 125 I am thy servant; give me understanding, that I may know thy testimonies.*

119:34

Only when we really understand can we do what God says. *34 Give me understanding, and I shall keep thy law; yea, I shall observe it with my whole heart.*

Nehemiah 8

The chapter describes the reading and explaining of the book of the law of Moses: *8 So they read in the book of the law of God distinctly, and gave the sense, and caused them to understand the reading . . . 12 And all the people went their way to eat, and to drink, and to send portions, and to make great mirth, because they had understood the words that were declared unto them*

Matthew 12:3, 7

Christ speaking: *3 Have ye not read what David did . . . ? 7 But if ye had known what this meaneth . . . ye would not have condemned the guiltless.*

Mark 7:14-18

*14 . . . He said . . . Hearken unto me every one of you, and understand . . . 16 If any man have ears to hear, let him hear . . . 18 . . . Are ye so without understanding also?*

See also 8:16-21;  10:2, 3;  12:24-26;  13:14

## 7. Public reading, especially of the Word of God, is a sound method of teaching. God's Word is effective!

Exodus 24:7

*And he [Moses] took the book of the covenant, and read in the audience of the people: and they said, All that the Lord hath said will we do, and be obedient.* God used the public reading to bring commitment to obey.

Joshua 8:34, 35   After the defeat and then victory over Ai: *34 . . . He read all the words of the law, the blessings and the cursings, according to all that is written in the book of the law* (See Deut. 28). *35 There was not a word of all that Moses commanded, which Joshua read not before all the congregation of Israel, with the women, and the little ones, and the strangers that were conversant among them.* Here the reading was an effective warning after the events they had just experienced.

2 Kings 22:8, 10-20;  23:1-25

An exciting account of the finding of the book of the Law in the temple  and reading of it to King Josiah and his repentance and concern to do God's will. Then followed the public reading (23:1-3), the King's covenant, and the people's agreement to it. The result was the destruction of idolatry in Israel and a great observance of the passover.

Jeremiah 36:4-25

Jeremiah called Baruch to write as he dictated (v. 4), and then to read in the temple the words of the Lord (5, 6). When Baruch read to the princes and advisors, they were afraid (14-19); they reported the message to King Jehoiakim who was so convicted by it that he cut it with a penknife and tossed it into the fire (20-25).

Because of his burning the book and refusing God's warning, God promised special judgment to the King - death, no burial, no heir on the throne (29-31).

Nehemiah 8:1-18

Here is the account of Ezra and others reading the law, after the return from captivity in Babylon. It was read over a seven-day period to men, women and children with results: understanding, sorrow for sin, rejoicing, worship, obedience, and more understanding. The whole chapter should be studied in showing the effects of reading the Word publicly.

Luke 4:16-21

Jesus read the Scriptures publicly: *16 And he came to Nazareth, where he had been brought up: and, as his custom was, he went into the synagogue on the sabbath day, and stood up for to read. 17 And there was delivered unto him the book of the prophet Esaias. And when he had opened the book, he found the place where it was written, 18 The Spirit of the Lord is upon me. . . .*

Colossians 4:16

Paul expected his epistles would be read in the churches: *16 And when this epistle is read among you, cause that it be read also in the church of the Laodiceans; and that ye likewise read the epistle from Laodicea.*

1 Thessalonians 5:27

*27 I charge you by the Lord that this epistle be read unto all the holy brethren.*

## 8. Public reading must be done well to be effective.

Nehemiah 8:1-18

In this passage several factors contribute to the effectiveness of the public reading. Note them as you study the passage:

(1) The people had a right attitude. They were gathered as one man (v. 1); they were attentive (3); they responded (6, 12, 14-17; also 9:1-3); they showed respect (5).

(2) They saw the Book of the Law from which the reading was done (2, 5).

(3) Ezra stood to read, had a pulpit or podium, and was on a raised platform so that people could see and hear (4, 5).

(4) Ezra was flanked by thirteen other men, who not only added to the impressiveness of the occasion, but helped to explain what was read (4, 7).

(5) Ezra himself worshipped the Lord, recognizing the significance of what he read (6); people responded to his example.

(6) The readers read distinctly and explained what they read (7, 8).

(7) The reading was continued over a period of time, with opportunity for response between the reading periods (9-18; also Chapter 9).

## 9. Excessive devotion to books is futile as well as tiresome. We can't know it all; we must be selective in what we read.

Ecclesiastes 12:12

Spoken when Solomon was an old man: *12 And further my son, be admonished: of making many books there is no end; and much study is a weariness of the flesh.*

(NASB) *But beyond this* (i.e., the importance of careful writing of v. 9-11) *my son, be warned: the writing of many books is endless, and excessive devotion to books is wearying to the body.*

John 21:25

*And there are also many other things which Jesus did,* *the which, if they should be written every one, I suppose that even the world itself could not contain the books that should be written.*

20:30, 31

*30 And many other signs truly did Jesus in the presence of his disciples, which are not written in this book: 31 But these are written that ye might believe that Jesus is the Christ, the Son of God; and that believing, ye might have life through his name.*

Also Luke 1:1-4;   1 John 2:1;   5:13.

## See also Chapters 3, 4, on writing and literature.

**TO ENCOURAGE THOUGHT ABOUT BOOKS:** Ask each pupil to design a suitable book jacket for a book recently read. Display around the room. Let each one stand by his design and give a brief "sales talk" about his book.

**TO SHOW VARIETY OF EFFECTS OF ONE BOOK:** Over a period of time read a book to children. Upon completion, ask each pupil to prepare a brief testimony telling what he liked best, or what part of the book had some influence on him.

# 3

## *Writing*

The Bible has a surprising amount to say about writing and its value. In addition, the Word itself demonstrates a variety of techniques, subjects, and styles of writing, all of which can serve as legitimate patterns for us.

Since writing is so closely related to reading and literature, additional help will be found in Chapters 2 and 4.

## CONCEPT SUMMARY

1. God recognizes writing as a powerful tool to influence people.
   a. God Himself wrote.
   b. God commanded others to write.
   c. God keeps records.
2. Written records enable us to know the past and learn from past events.
3. Written prophecy enables us to recognize events as part of God's plan.
4. Written doctrine and standards make consistency possible from person to person and from generation to generation.
5. The use of written materials in teaching makes it possible for learners to review what has been presented in other ways, and to study it more deeply.
6. God has used writers down through history to accomplish His purposes.
7. Many kinds of writing are used by God for His purposes.
8. Writing may deal with a variety of subjects and be valuable from God's viewpoint.
9. Writing that follows God's plan makes use of numerous techniques.
10. There are times when writing is better than speaking.
11. Effective writing demands careful research, documentation, and wise expression.
12. Writing should be clear and legible.

# SCRIPTURAL BACKGROUND

## 1. God recognizes writing as a powerful tool to influence people.

### a. God Himself wrote.

Exodus 31:18

*And he [God] gave unto Moses, when he had made an end of communing with him upon mount Sinai, two tables of testimony, tables of stone, written with the finger of God.*

32:16

*And the tables were the work of God, and the writing was the writing of God, graven upon the tables.*

34:1

*And the Lord said unto Moses, Hew thee two tables of stone like unto the first: and I will write upon these tables the words that were in the first tables, which thou brakest.*

Daniel 5:5, 25-28

God to Belshazzar: *5 In the same hour came forth fingers of a man's hand, and wrote . . . and the king saw the part of the hand that wrote . . . . 25 And this was the writing that was written . . . 26 This is the interpretation of the thing: MENE; God hath numbered thy kingdom, and finished it. 27 TEKEL; Thou art weighed in the balances, and art found wanting. 28 PERES; Thy kingdom is divided, and given to the Medes and Persians.*

### b. God commanded others to write.

Exodus 17:14

The account of victory over Amalek: *14 And the Lord said unto* <u>Moses</u>*, Write this for a memorial in a book, and and rehearse it in the ears of Joshua . . . .*

34:27, 28

*27 And the Lord said unto* <u>Moses</u>*, Write thou these words: for after the tenor of these words I have made a covenant with thee and with Israel. 28 And he was there with the Lord forty days and forty nights. . . .*

*And he wrote upon the tables the words of the covenant, the ten commandments.*

Deuteronomy 6:6-9

*6 And these words, which I command thee this day, shalt be in thine heart; 7 And thou shalt teach them . . . 8 And thou shalt bind them . . . 9 And thou shalt write them upon the posts of thy house, and on thy gates.*

Here was a command for <u>parents</u> to write parts of the word of God.

17:18-20

God's command to Israel's future <u>king</u>: *18 And it shall be, when he sitteth upon the throne of his kingdom, that he shall write him a copy of this law in a book out of that which is before the priests the Levites.* God's reasoning is given in verses 19, 20.

31:19, 21, 22

The Lord speaking to <u>Moses</u>: *19 Now therefore write ye this song for you, and teach it the children of Israel: put it in their mouths, that this song may be a witness for me against the children of Israel.*

Jeremiah 30:2

God speaking to <u>Jeremiah</u>: *2 Thus speaketh the Lord God of Israel, saying, Write thee all the words that I have spoken unto thee in a book.*

See also 36:2, 27, 28; Ezekiel 43:11.

Revelation 1:11, 19

Christ to the Apostle <u>John</u>: *11 . . . What thou seest, write in a book, and send it unto the seven churches which are in Asia . . . 19 Write the things which thou hast seen, and the things which are, and the things which shall be hereafter.*

See also 2:1, 8, 12, 18; 3:1, 7, 14; 19:9; 21:5.

**c. God keeps records. Though they may not be literally written on paper with a pen, they are pictured to us in this fashion.**

<u>The Book of Life</u>

Philippians 4:3

Paul writing: *I entreat thee . . . help those women . . . with Clement also, and with other my fellowlabourers, whose names are in the book of life.*

Revelation 20:15

*And whosoever was not found written in the book of life was cast into the lake of fire.*

See also Ex. 32:32, 33; Psa. 69:28; Luke 10:20; Rev. 3:5; 13:8; 17:8; 20:12; 21:27; 22:19.

<u>The Books</u> (record of works of those not trusting Christ)

Revelation 20:12

*And I saw the dead, small and great, stand before God; and the books were opened: and another book was opened which is the book of life: and the dead were judged out of those things which were written in the books, according to their works.*

<u>Book of Remembrance</u>

Malachi 3:16

*Then they that feared the Lord spake often one to another: and the Lord hearkened and heard it, and a book of remembrance was written before him for them that feared the Lord, and that thought upon his name.*

See also Psa. 56:8; 139:16.

**2. Written records enable us to know the past and learn from past events.**

Psalm 102:18

*This shall be written for the generation to come and the people which shall be created shall praise the Lord.*

Isaiah 30:8-11

*8 Now go, write it before them in a table, and note it in a book, that it may be for the time to come for ever and ever: 9 That this is a rebellious people, lying children, children that will not hear the Law of the Lord.*

Luke 1:1-4

The reason for the Gospel of Luke: *1 Forasmuch as many have taken in hand to set forth in order a declaration of those things which are most surely believed among us, 2 Even as they delivered them unto us, which from the beginning were eyewitnesses . . . 3 It seemed good to me also . . . to write unto thee in order . . . 4 That thou mightest know the certainty of those things, wherein thou hast been instructed.*

Romans 15:4

*For whatsoever things were written aforetime were written for our learning . . . .*

1 Corinthians 10:6, 11

*6 Now these things were our examples, to the intent we should not lust after evil things, as they also lusted. 11 Now all these things happened unto them for ensamples: and they are written for our admonition upon whom the ends of the world are come.*

<u>Examples</u>

Ezra 4:7-24  The use of records of Israel's history of rebelliousness in stopping the rebuilding of the temple; Israel's records were used by their enemies! See especially verses 15, 19-21.

Nehemiah 7:5, 6

Nehemiah speaking: *5 And my God put into mine heart to gather together the nobles, and the rulers, and the people, that they might be reckoned by genealogy. And I found a register of the genealogy of them which came up at the first, and found written therein, 6 These are the children of the province, that went up out of the captivity, of those that had been carried away, whom Nebuchadnezzar the king of Babylon had carried away, and came again to Jerusalem . . .*Then follows the list.

The records disallowed some who also wanted to be included, as noted in verses 61, 64, 65.

Esther 6, 7

Here is the account of the way in which the king's hearing the reading of the book of records of his kingdom caused him to realize that Mordecai merited honor for earlier saving his life; as a result the tables were turned on Haman and the Jews were saved.

PROJECT: In the Book of Ezekiel, note the many times that he mentions specific dates when the Lord spoke to him. Ezekiel must have kept a diary. Note this same kind of recording dates in other books, especially in the historical books.

## 3. Written prophecy enables us to recognize events as part of God's plan.

Isaiah 8:1-4

God speaking to Isaiah: *1 . . . Take thee a great roll, and write in it with a man's pen concerning Maher-shalal-hash-baz . . . 3 And I went unto the prophetess; and she conceived, and bare a son. Then said the Lord to me, Call his name Maher-shalal-hash-baz. 4 For before the child shall have knowledge to cry, My father and my mother, the riches of Damascus and the spoil of Samaria shall be taken away by the king of Assyria.*

Here God was telling of a future event, soon to occur, so soon that Isaiah's son would not yet be able to call his parents by name. The name given to Isaiah's son means in the Hebrew, "Swift is the booty, speedy is the prey." God indicated the time of this judgment specifically enough so that Israel would recognize it.

48:3-5

God speaking to Israel: *3 I have declared the former things from the beginning; and they went forth out of my mouth, and I shewed them; I did them suddenly, and they came to pass, 4 Because I knew that thou art obstinate . . . 5 I have even from the beginning declared it to thee; before it came to pass I shewed it thee: lest thou shouldest say, Mine idol hath done them . . . .*

Jeremiah 29:1-10

*1 Now these are the words of the letter that Jeremiah the prophet sent from Jerusalem unto . . . all the people whom Nebuchadnezzar had carried away captive from Jerusalem to Babylon . . . 4 Thus saith the Lord . . . 5 Build houses . . . plant gardens . . . 6 Take ye wives, and beget sons and daughters . . . that ye may be increased there, and not diminished . . . 10 For thus saith the Lord, That after seventy years be accomplished at Babylon I will visit you, and perform my good word toward you, in causing you to return to this place.*

30:2, 3

*2 Thus speaketh the Lord God of Israel, saying, Write thee all the words that I have spoken unto thee in a book. 3 For, lo, the days come, saith the Lord, that I will bring again the captivity of my people Israel and and Judah, saith the Lord: and I will cause them to return to the land that I gave to their fathers, and they shall possess it.*

32:6-44

Babylon had already besieged Jerusalem (v. 2), and Jeremiah was in prison by act of Judah's king. In spite of these discouraging facts, in obedience to God, Jeremiah bought a field and was careful to record the transaction legally because God had promised the Jews would return to their land. The written record would evidence the transaction and Jeremiah's faith in God's promise.

Daniel 9:2-4

*2 In the first year of his reign I Daniel understood by books the number of the years, whereof the word of the Lord came to Jeremiah the prophet, that he would accomplish seventy years in the desolations of Jerusalem.* (See Jeremiah 25:11-13) *3 And I set my face unto the Lord God . . . 4 And I prayed . . . .*

9:13

Daniel still speaking: *As it is written in the law of Moses, all this evil is come upon us . . . .*

In these two passages, Daniel acknowledges the fact that it was because Moses and Jeremiah wrote the messages of the Lord, and he read them, that he had an understanding of the times in which he lived and was therefore able to proceed properly.

Luke 24:25-27

Christ with two disciples on the road to Emmaus: *25 Then he said unto them, O fools and slow of heart to believe all that the prophets have spoken: 26 Ought not Christ to have suffered these things, and to enter into his glory? 27 And beginning at Moses and all the prophets, he expounded unto them in all the scriptures the things concerning himself.*

See also verses 44-48. The Lord expected them to recognize the truth of what had happened to Him because of the written prophecies.

Acts 13:32-27

Paul speaking: *32 And we declare unto you glad tidings, how that the promise which was made unto the fathers, 33 God hath fulfilled the same unto us their children, in that he hath raised up Jesus again; as it is also written in the second psalm, Thou art my Son, this day have I begotten thee. 34 And as concerning that he raised him up from the dead, now no more to return to corruption, he said on this wise, I will give you the sure mercies of David. 35 Wherefore he saith also in another psalm, Thou shalt not suffer thine Holy One to see corruption.* See Psalm 2:7 and 16:10.

Paul expected that these men who had gathered in the synagogue, as noted in verses 14, 15, would know the written prophecies and recognize Christ as their fulfillment.

## 4. Written doctrine and standards make consistency possible from person to person, from generation to generation.

Examples

Exodus 24:3, 4, 7, 12

*3 And Moses . . . told the people all the words of the Lord and all the judgments . . . 4 And Moses wrote all the words of the Lord . . . 7 And he took the book of the covenant and read in the audience of the people: and they said, All that the Lord hath said will we do, and be obedient. 12 The Lord said unto Moses . . . I will give thee tables of stone, and a law, and commandments which I have written; that thou mayest teach them.*

Deuteronomy 27:2-8

God records the fact that just before Israel crossed the Jordan River to enter Canaan, Moses charged the people thus: *2 . . . Thou shalt set thee up great stones . . . 3 And thou shalt write upon them all the words of this law . . . 4 . . . when ye be gone over Jordan, that ye shall set up these stones . . . in mount Ebal . . . 8 And thou shalt write upon the stones all the words of this law very plainly.*

Esther 9:25-32

The setting up of the days of Purim - a celebration of victory: *27 The Jews ordained, and took upon them, and upon their seed . . . that they would keep these two days according to their writing . . . 28 And that these days should be remembered throughout every generation, every family, every province, and every city; and that these days of Purim should not fail from among the Jews, nor the memorial of them perish from their seed. 29 Then Esther the queen . . . wrote with all authority, to confirm this second letter of Purim. . . .*

Acts 15:23-29

Letter to the church at Antioch after the council at the Jerusalem church: *23 And they wrote letters by them after this manner . . . : 25 It seemed good unto us, being assembled with one accord, to send chosen men unto you with our beloved Barnabas and Paul . . . 28 For it seemed good to the Holy Ghost, and to us, to lay upon you no greater burden than these necessary things; 29 That ye abstain from meats offered to idols, and from blood, and from things strangled, and from fornication: from which if ye keep yourselves, ye shall do well. Fare ye well.*

## 5. The use of written materials in teaching makes it possible for learners to review what has been presented in other ways, and to study it more deeply.

Luke 1:1-4

Luke's reason for writing his Gospel: *1 Forasmuch as many have taken in hand to set forth . . . those things which are most surely believed among us . . . 3 It seemed good to me also . . . to write unto thee in order, most excellent Theophilus, 4 That thou mightest know the certainty of those things, wherein thou hast been instructed.*

1 Corinthians 4:14-17

Paul wrote to warn the Corinthians, recognizing the fact that he was their spiritual father, the one through whom they had been saved. He did this to supplement what Timothy would do in personal teaching when he would visit them.

Ephesians 3:3, 4

Here too Paul says that he wrote to them what God had revealed so they could understand his knowledge. He had previously visited them and taught them.

Colossians 4:7-9

Paul was willing that Tychicus and Onesimus should convey to the church the news concerning himself, but he was careful to write the teaching which he was to give them - the main body of this epistle. *7 All my state shall Tychicus declare unto you . . . 8 Whom I have sent unto you . . . 9 With Onesimus . . . They shall make known unto you all things which are done here.*

2 Peter 3:1, 2

*1 This second epistle, beloved, I now write unto you, in both which I stir up your pure minds by way of remembrance: 2 That ye may be mindful of the words which were spoken before by the holy prophets, and of the commandment of us the apostles of the Lord and Savior.*

3:15, 16

Peter was able to reenforce his own writing with the writings of the Apostle Paul.

See also Ecclesiastes 12:9-12, for Solomon's view of the importance of written materials for teaching.

## 6. God has used writers down through history to accomplish His purposes.

Examples

Moses, in the writing of the Pentateuch, giving us both the Law and the early history of the world, the race, Israel.

The record-keepers and the history writers used by God to produce the Historical Books. Here we have the history of Israel, both in the land and during the Babylonian Captivity, and the story of the rebuilding after 70 years.

David, Solomon and others, to whom we owe the Poetical Books, with all of their worship and wisdom.

The Prophets who recorded their prophecies, along with the Lord's dealings with them.

The Gospel-writers who gave us details of the earthly ministry and the teachings of Christ, followed by the record of the early church, in the Book of Acts.

Paul, James, Peter, and the Apostle John, who wrote teaching letters to churches and individuals, plus the record of what John saw of the future, recorded in the Revelation.

The Church Fathers, who gave us detailed accounts of the ways in which the early church thought and acted.

The Reformation writers who spread the emphasis on the Bible as the authority for Christian life and church practice.

PROJECT: Look for the word *write* in a Bible concordance. Find passages where God commanded someone to write. Prepare your findings in chart form, using these headings: BIBLE REFERENCE, PERSON TO WHOM COMMAND WAS GIVEN, CIRCUMSTANCES, WHAT HE WAS TO WRITE.

PROJECT: Choose outstanding modern writers who have been used by the Lord in an unusual way and assign certain ones for reports showing their influence.

PROJECT: Select a few outstanding writers who, by their writings, have influenced people toward wrong purposes or actions. Study the extent of their influence.

PROJECT: Select classics which have been widely read and which have had influence for good. Determine the major message(s) of each book; gather facts concerning the extent of the circulation of the book and the period of time over which it has exerted an influence. Examples: *Pilgrim's Progress*, the *New England Primer*, *McGuffey's Readers*, *Robinson Crusoe*. For *Robinson Crusoe*, be sure to obtain the Moody Press edition which is a copy of the original.

## 7. Many kinds of writing are used by God for His purposes.

Examples

Historical writing, which gives the facts, often in narrative form, as in the Pentateuch, Historical Books, Gospels, Acts.

Lists, genealogies, land distribution records, etc., as in Genesis 10; Numbers 1-10; Nehemiah 7, 11, 12; Matthew 1; Luke 3:23-38.

Poetry, as in the Psalms, but also in such passages as Exodus 15; Deuteronomy 31:19-22 and Chapter 32;

2 Samuel 22. Also the Book of Job, Ecclesiastes, Song of Solomon, and parts of Major and Minor Prophets. See the New American Standard Version for a clearer showing of poetic portions of Scripture.

Proverbs, especially in the Book of Proverbs, but many can be found elsewhere in Scripture. 1 Kings 4:32 records with God's approval the fact that Solomon wrote 3000 proverbs, and 1005 songs. Ecclesiastes 12:9-12 describes the care with which he wrote them.

Letters, as in the Epistles, and in Revelation 2, 3.

Sermons and oral discourses, as in the Sermon on the Mount, the Olivet Discourse (Matt. 24, 25), Peter's sermon on the Day of Pentecost (Acts 2), his address to the Sanhedrin (Acts 4:5-12), Stephen's address before the council (Acts 7), Peter's sermon in the home of Cornelius (Acts 10:34-43), Paul's defence (Acts 22), his appeal to Agrippa (Acts 26).

Exhortations, all through Scripture.

## 8. Writing may deal with a variety of subjects and be valuable from God's viewpoint.

The example presented in the Bible shows God's concern about every topic which relates to life. The Bible does not limit itself to the presentation of how we can be related to Him - the vertical relationship. Instead God used His writers, moved by the Holy Spirit, to write His teachings concerning all of life - physical, mental, moral, emotional, social, spiritual, family - or however we may wish to divide it.

God has seen to it that His views on every school subject are recorded for our study. For example, He has written on science, history, social relationships, money, leadership, speech, health. The present volume, as well as others in this series, is designed to bring together for the teacher a compilation of Biblical teachings, organized according to school subjects.

Surely the implication is that God is related to all of life; He has shown that concern by His writings; we too should be challenged to study and write on a variety of subjects, always evaluating our thoughts by His Word.

## 9. Writing that follows God's pattern makes use of numerous techniques.

Examples

Similes and Metaphors:

Jeremiah 1:18

Jeremiah is likened to a fortified city, an iron pillar and a bronze wall.

2:2

Judah is spoken of as a betrothed maiden.

2:13

God refers to Himself as the *fountain of living waters,* and to other gods as *broken cisterns that can hold no water.*

2:18

God refers to Judah's dependence on Egypt and Assyria as *drinking the waters of the Nile,* and *drinking the waters of the Euphrates* (NASB).

2:20, 24

God refers to Judah's unfaithfulness to Him as *playing the harlot,* and as *a wild ass used to the wilderness, that snuffeth up the wind at her pleasure.* (NASB uses the expression in verse 24: *the passion of a wild donkey seeking a mate.*) See also 3:1, 6-10, 20 and many other passages where the unfaithfulness of Israel of Judah is likened to marital unfaithfulness.

Contrasts

Jeremiah 2:32-36

God contrasts the careful attention a bride gives to her ornaments, her dress and all the details of her wedding to the careless way His people treat Him.

2:2-8

God contrasts the early days of Israel when they went after Him in the wilderness, and *Israel was holiness unto the Lord, and the firstfruits of his increase* (v. 3) with the later days of Israel, when even the priests, pastors and prophets didn't know Him (v. 8).

References to authority - i.e., to the Law, the Prophets, the Psalms

Matthew 11:10

Jesus to the multitude about John the Baptist:

*10 For this is he, of whom it is written, Behold, I send my messenger before thy face* . . . . Also Mark 1:2, 3.

Romans 1:17

*For therein is the righteousness of God revealed from faith to faith: as it is written, The just shall live by faith.*

Also 1 Cor. 1:19; 2:9, and many other references.

Quotations and Allusions

Consider the many passages where the expressions *it is written,* and *as it is written* introduce a statement. Use a concordance.

Also, Nave's Topical Bible lists more than seven pages of quotations and allusions to the Old Testament, repeated in the New Testament. Here is a valuable source for this kind of study.

Rhetorical Questions (Jeremiah is full of them; so is Paul.)

Jeremiah 2:5

> *5 Thus saith the Lord, What iniquity have your fathers found in me, that they are gone far from me, and have walked after vanity, and are become vain?*

2:11, 14, 17

> *11 Hath a nation changed their gods, which are yet no gods? 14 Is Israel a servant? is he a homeborn slave? why is he spoiled? 17 Hast thou not procured this unto thyself, in that thou hast forsaken the Lord thy God, when he led thee by the way?*

See also Rom. 8:31-35; 9:14, 19-24, etc.; 2 Pet. 3:11, 12.

Parables

Judges 9:8-15  The trees choosing a king.
2 Samuel 12:1-6  Nathan's parable of the lamb.
Matthew 13  Parables of the Kingdom.
Luke 10:30-37  The Good Samaritan.
See Nave's <u>Topical Bible</u> for a more complete listing.
> Look under the headings: Parables; Jesus the Christ, Parables of.

## 10.  There are times when writing is better than speaking.

Acts 15:20  At the council at Jerusalem:  It was decided that a letter be written, rather than leaving the conveying of the decision to the memory of the messengers.

2 Corinthians 13:10

> *Therefore I write these things being absent, lest being present I should use sharpness, according to the power which the Lord hath given me to edification, and not to destruction.* (Also v. 2)

Here Paul was concerned that he say what would help, not hinder, the saints.

## 11.  Effective writing demands careful research, documentation, and wise expression.

Ecclesiastes 12:9-12

> *9 . . . Because the preacher was wise, he still taught the people knowledge; yea, he gave good heed, and sought out, and set in order many proverbs. 10 The preacher sought to find out acceptable words: and that which was written was upright, even words of truth. 11 The words of the wise are as goads, and as nails fastened by the masters of assemblies, which are given from one shepherd. 12 And further, by these, my son, be admonished: of making many books there is no end; and much study is a weariness of the flesh.*

Here is the testimony of the wisest man, one to whom God had given special wisdom, and whom He used to do considerable writing which was to be His Word. Even Solomon says, "It's hard work to write!"

PROJECT: Many of the writers of Scripture were extremely careful to keep before their readers the authority behind what they were saying and writing. Watch this especially in the messages of the prophets, such as Jeremiah and Ezekiel, but in others as well. They gave credit.

## 12.  Writing should be clear and legible.

See especially Deuteronomy 27:8 and Habakkuk 2:2, but consider also other Scripture cited on pages 7 and 8.

"A man who writes an immoral but immortal book may be tracked into eternity by a procession of lost souls from every generation, every one to be a witness against him at the judgment, to show to him and to the universe the immeasurableness of his iniquity."

> **George B. Cheever**
> **1807-1890**

"There are only two powers in the world, the sword and the pen; and in the end the former is always conquered by the latter."

> **Napoleon Bonaparte**
> **1769-1821**

# 4

## Literature

## CONCEPT SUMMARY

1. **The Bible is great literature.**

   **Test No. 1:** **PERMANENCE.** The Bible has stood the test of time.

   **Test No. 2:** **UNIVERSALITY.** The Bible has universal appeal and therefore has been widely distributed.

   **Test No. 3:** **ARTISTRY.** The Bible demonstrates the artistry of God's blending together His chosen personalities to present through their word pictures His single eternal canvas.

   **Test No. 4:** **EMOTIONAL APPEAL.** The Bible appeals to the emotions and the imagination as well as to the intellect.

   **Test No. 5:** **INDIVIDUAL STYLE.** The Bible exhibits styles of writing which, though they express the message of God without error, show the personalities of the human writers.

2. **The Bible in its use of many styles and types of writing provides patterns for modern writers.**

3. **The teachings of the Bible furnish the criteria by which we must judge the truth and wholesomeness of other writings.**

4. The authority of the Bible supersedes that of other literature: it must therefore be approached with a different attitude.

5. Because the Bible is God's Word, we need not expect to understand it completely.

6. The Bible has molded much of the thinking and literature of man; therefore we cannot understand much of literature without Bible knowledge.

7. Man's writings reflect his inner thoughts and desires; therefore we study literature to understand people.

8. Our minds much be constantly filled with that which is pure and wholesome. We are responsible for those things with which we fill our minds.

9. Not all literature is good. Some should be avoided entirely - even burned; other should be read with careful discernment.

10. Knowledge of non-Christian literature may be used by God in His service.

## QUOTES TO QUOTE

If religious books are not widely circulated among the masses in this country, and the people do not become religious, I do not know what is to become of us as a nation . . . . . . . . . . . . . . . . . . . . . . . . . . . . . . . . . . . . . . . .

If truth be not diffused, error will be; if God and his word are not known and received, the devil and his works will gain the ascendance; if the evangelical volume does not reach every hamlet, the pages of a corrupt and licentious literature will; if the power of the Gospel is not felt through the length and breadth of the land, anarchy and misrule, degradation and misery, corruption and darkness, will reign without mitigation or end.

-- Daniel Webster
1782-1852

The book to read is not the one which thinks for you, but the one which makes you think. No book in the world equals the Bible for that.

-- James McCosh
1811-1894

Upon books the collective education of the race depends; they are the sole instruments of registering, perpetuating, and transmitting thought.

-- H. Rogers
1806-1877

Think as well as read . . . . Yield not your minds to the passive impressions which others may make upon them. Hear what they have to say; but examine it, weigh it, and judge for yourselves. This will enable you to make a right use of books -- to use them as helpers, not as guides to your understanding; as counsellors, not as dictators of what you are to think and believe.

-- Tryon Edwards
1809-1894

## SCRIPTURAL BACKGROUND

### 1. The Bible is great literature.

### Test No. 1: PERMANENCE. The Bible has endured the test of time.

a. God said this would be true.

Psalm 119:89

*Forever, O Lord, thy word is settled in heaven.*

119:100

David's testimony that what he learned from the law of the Lord stood the test of time: *100 I understand more than the ancients, because I keep thy precepts.*

Deuteronomy 17:18-20

Here God used Moses, 1451 B.C., to speak of the value or permanence of the Law of God for an event that was not to take place for 350 years.  1 Samuel 10:1.

b. History has proven it true.

Though the early parts of the Bible were written back in the time of Moses (1571-1431 B.C.) and Job (1530 B.C.) and other parts over a period of time extending up to about A.D. 96 for the Revelation, the Bible is still being sold and read by millions of people who find satisfaction in it.

### Test No. 2: UNIVERSALITY. The Bible has universal appeal and therefore has been widely distributed.

It is generally agreed that good literature begets response from people with varying backgrounds and cultures. Because it deals with the common experiences of man, it is not limited to one culture or one age. The Bible presents such themes as good and evil, God and sin, guilt and salvation, inter-personal relationships, life after death - themes with which everyone has some concern.

a. God promised wide distribution for His message.

Psalm 108:3

*. . . I will sing praises unto thee among the nations.*

Though David was from Judah, he expected that his psalms would reach into other nations.

Jeremiah 1:5

God speaking to Jeremiah: . . . *Before thou camest out of the womb, I sanctified thee, and I ordained thee a prophet unto the nations.* Though Jeremiah had a special ministry to Judah just before and during the Captivity, God specifically ordained that his message would have a wider distribution.

Matthew 28:19, 20

Here the Lord Jesus Christ commissions his disciples

to 19 *Go ye therefore and teach all nations, baptizing…* *20 Teaching them to observe all things whatsoever I have commanded you.*

24:14

Speaking of the coming Kingdom, Christ promised: *14 This gospel of the kingdom shall be preached in all the world for a witness unto all nations.* Also Mark 13:10.

Acts 9:15

God promised Ananias that Paul was to bear His name before the Gentile nations, before kings, and before Israel. Also 1 Timothy 2:7; 2 Timothy 1:11; 4:17.

b. History shows the universal appeal and the resultant wide distribution of the Bible.

The most valuable printed books are copies of the Gutenberg Bible, printed in 1455 as the earliest mechanically printed full length books. Copies have sold for as much as two and a half billion dollars. [1]

According to the 1980 edition of Guiness Book of World Records, portions of the Bible have been translated into 1659 languages, compared with 222 languages for the writings of Lenin. Copies printed between 1800 and 1950 are estimated at 1½ billion. [1]

The Bible has been the best seller among non-fiction books on many different occasions. For instance, several times recently one particular version was the top seller for the year: the Revised Standard Version in 1952, 1953, 1954; the New English Bible, New Testament in 1961; the Living Bible in 1972, 1973. [2]

## Test No. 3: ARTISTRY. The Bible demonstrates the artistry of God's blending together His chosen personalities to present through their word pictures His single eternal canvas.

The Bible displays the art of choosing the right words and putting them together in a way that stimulates the reader's appetite to keep reading the vital message the Author wants him to understand, appreciate and act upon. Each of the sixty-six books has its own peculiar message to convey, and each stands on its own as a work of art. The Bible, unlike any other book, goes much further in its artistry by weaving the diverse backgrounds and vocabularies of the human writers to present one grand mural of the ages.

Consider the concepts presented in Chapter 3, WRITING, Concepts 7, 8, 9, on pages 23-25.

Consider also some of the great themes which run through the whole Bible, despite its many human writers. For instance, creation, the greatness of God,

man's need for God, the all-sufficient Christ, judgment for sin, a coming kingdom when Messiah shall reign, Heaven.

PROJECT: Using a topical Bible, or even a concordance, find passages from various books of the Bible which deal with some of the above themes, or others of your own choosing. Nave's Topical Bible is helpful for many studies.

PROJECT: Make a list of the various human writers of the Bible, along with what information you can find about their occupation or experience. Note the unusual variety in their backgrounds. Use a Bible encyclopedia for help in finding the facts about the persons involved, but use also the Bible itself.

## Test No. 4: EMOTIONAL APPEAL. The Bible appeals to the emotions and the imagination as well as to the intellect.

One of the functions of literature is the enjoyment it brings to the reader. Though the Bible provides much instruction, it does more than that. Much of its teaching is done through experience. Instead of talking about a truth or a virtue, the writers have portrayed that truth in action.

The Bible surely does more than delight us, but it does

that, if we know Him and accept it for what it is. In fact, even many who do not accept the inerrancy of the Bible and the divine Authorship delight in parts of the Bible, purely from its emotional appeal. Testimonies appear in the Bible itself concerning the pleasure that comes from reading its pages and meditating on its truth. For example:

---

[1] Norris McWhirter, *Guinness Book of World Records* (N. Y.: Sterling Publishers, 1980).

[2] *Reader's Digest Almanac and Yearbook* (W. W. Norton, Co., 1979), p. 92.

Psalm 1:1, 2

Here the blessed or happy man is described as one whose *"delight is in the law of the Lord, and he meditates therein day and night."*

119:24

*Thy testimonies also are my delight and my counsellors.*

119:77, 97

*77 . . . Thy law is my delight. 97 O how I love thy law! it is my meditation all the day.* Also v. 174.

119:92

*Unless thy law had been my delights, I should then have perished in mine affliction.*

119:143

*Trouble and anguish have taken hold on me: yet thy commandments are my delights.* Also v. 47, 48.

119:103

*How sweet are thy words unto my taste! yea sweeter than honey to my mouth!*

19:8-10

*8 The statutes of the Lord are right, rejoicing the heart . . . 9 . . . the judgments of the Lord are true and righteous altogether. 10 More to be desired are they than gold, yea, than much fine gold: sweeter also than honey and the honeycomb.*

## Test No. 5: INDIVIDUAL STYLE. The Bible exhibits styles of writing which, though they express the message of God without error, show the personalities of the human writers.

a. The control of God, that His message be given without error.

2 Peter 1:20, 21

*20 . . . No prophecy of the scripture is of any private-interpretation* [origination]. *21 For the prophecy came not in old time by the will of man: but holy men of God spake as they were moved* [or, borne along] *by the Holy Ghost.*

2 Timothy 3:16, 17

*All scripture is given by inspiration* [or, outbreathing] *of God, and is profitable for doctrine, for reproof, for correction, for instruction in righteousness: 17 That the man of God may be perfect, throughly furnished unto all good works.*

b. The personality of the human writers who were thus controlled.

Consider, for example, the differences in style and emphasis between the writings of the apostles Peter and Paul. Paul begins each epistle with some of the great doctrinal truths of Christianity, then follows with a section showing how to apply these truths to life. In contrast, Peter intersperses the doctrinal and the practical.

Matthew writes with the Jews in mind, quoting much from the Old Testament showing that Jesus is the Messiah. Mark emphasizes the servant aspect of Christ's life on earth, with great brevity and forthrightness. After

detailing the birth of Christ so there would be no question concerning the supernaturalness of it, Luke shows the human-ness of the Son of God. John's approach is different still, with its emphasis on those sayings and actions of the Lord that show Him to be God.

Some of the writers are very specific in stating the purpose of their writing; others are not. The Apostle John writes *"that ye might believe that Jesus is the Christ, the Son of God; and that believing ye might have life through his name"* (John 20:31). In his epistle, he writes to those who already believe, with concern that they know that they have eternal life (1 John 5:13).

Luke, as an eyewitness to the events in the life of our Lord, shows his concern that his readers *"know the certainty of those things, wherein* [they] *have been instructed* (Luke 1:4). He further explains what he intended to include, when he says, in Acts 1:1, 2, that he wrote *"of all that Jesus began both to do and teach"* until His ascension.

Though many of the human writers do not spell out their purposes, a careful reading makes them clear. And they are not all the same.

## 2. The Bible in its use of many styles and types of writing provides patterns for modern writers.

See Chapter 3, WRITING, Concepts 7, 8, 9, pages 23-25.

### 3. The teachings of the Bible furnish the criteria by which we must judge the truth and wholesomeness of other writings.

See Chapter 1, LANGUAGE ARTS AND ENGLISH IN GENERAL, Concept 9, page 7.

### 4. The authority of the Bible supersedes that of other literature; it must therefore be approached with a different attitude.

See Chapter 2, READING, Concepts 3,4,5, pages 13,14.

It may be helpful at this point for the teacher to have a succinct statement concerning why we believe the Bible is the Word of God - i.e., how we know it is different from other books. The following reasons are those listed by Dr. R. A. Torrey in *Our Bible*, copyrighted in 1898 by Moody Press, Moody Bible Institute, and used by permission:

a. First, on the ground of the testimony of Jesus Christ. Mark 7:13; Luke 24:27; John 10:35; 14:26; 16:13, 14.

b. Second, on the ground of its fulfilled prophecies. Torrey speaks of two kind of prophecies in the Bible - the explicit prophecies about the Jews, the nations, and the Messiah; and the Old Testament events, institutions and ceremonies which are called types and which portray in picture something future.

c. Third, on the ground of the unity of the book.
"The Bible consists of 66 books, written by more than thirty different men, extending in the period of its composition over more than fifteen hundred years; written in three different languages, in many different countries, and by men on every plane of social life, from the herdman and fisherman and cheap politician up to the king upon his throne; written under all sorts of circumstances; yet in all this wonderful conglomeration we find an absolute unity of thought." (*Our Bible*, p. 120)

d. Fourth, on the ground of the immeasurable superiority of the teachings of the Bible to those of any other and all other books.

(1) The Bible has in it nothing but truth, while all the others have truth mixed with error.

(2) The Bible contains all truth.
"There is not a truth to be found anywhere on moral or spiritual subjects that you cannot find in substance within the covers of that old Book." (*Our Bible*, p. 122)

(3) The Bible contains more truth than all other books together.

e. Fifth, on the ground of the history of the book, its victory over attack.

"This book has always been hated. No sooner was it given to the world than it met the hatred of men, and they tried to stamp it out. Celsus tried it by the brilliancy of his genius, Porphyry by the depth of his philosophy; but they failed. Lucian directed against it the shafts of his ridicule, Diocletian the power of the Roman empire; but they failed. Edicts backed by all the power of the empire were issued that every Bible should be burned, and that everyone who had a Bible should be put to death. For eighteen centuries every engine of destruction that human science, philosophy, wit, reasoning or brutality could bring to bear against a book has been brought to bear against that book to stamp it out of the world, but it has a mightier hold on the world today [1898] than ever before." (*Our Bible*, p. 123)

f. Sixth, on the ground of the character of those who accept and of those who reject the book.

g. Seventh, on the ground of the influence of the book.

"There is more power in that little book to save men, and purify, gladden and beautify their lives, than in all other literature put together - more power to lift men up to God." (*Our Bible*, p. 125)

h. Eighth, on the ground of the inexhaustible depth of the book.

"Nothing has been added to it in eighteen hundred years, yet a man like Bunsen, or Neander, cannot exhaust it by the study of a lifetime. George Mueller read it through more than one hundred times, and said it was fresher every time he read it. Could that be true of any other book?" (*Our Bible*, p. 127)

i. Ninth, on the ground of the fact that as we grow in knowledge and holiness we grow toward the Bible.

j. Tenth, on the ground of the direct testimony of the Holy Spirit.

"The Holy Spirit sets His seal in the soul of every believer to the Divine authority of the Bible. It is possible to get to a place where we need no argument to prove that the Bible is God's Word. Christ says, *'My sheep know my voice,'* and God's children know His voice . . .". (*Our Bible*, p. 129)

## 5. Because the Bible is God's Word, we need not expect to understand it completely.

Deuteronomy 29:29

*The secret things belong unto the Lord our God: but those things which are revealed belong unto us and to our children forever, that we may do all the words of this law.*

Isaiah 55:8, 9

*8 For my thoughts are not your thoughts, neither are your ways my ways, saith the Lord. 9 For as the* *heavens are higher than the earth, so are my ways higher than your ways, and my thoughts than your thoughts.*

Romans 11:33

*O the depth of the riches both of the wisdom and knowledge of God! How unsearchable are his judgments, and his ways past finding out!*

## 6. The Bible has molded much of thinking and literature of man; therefore we cannot understand much of literature without Bible knowledge.

"The Bible is like the banyan tree; its very branches bend down and take root. It spreads over whole continents, and could not be eradicated without tearing up the very soil of society.

"The contents of the Scriptures have supplied themes for the greatest poets, artists and musicians which the world has yet produced, and have been the mightiest factor of all in shaping the moral progress of the race. Let us consider a few examples of the Bible's influence as displayed in the various realms of human enterprise.

"Take away such sublime oratorios as *Elijah* and The *Messiah* and you have taken out of the realm of music something which can never be duplicated; destroy the countless hymns which have drawn their inspiration from the Scriptures and you have left us little else worth singing. Eliminate from the compositions of Tennyson, Wordsworth and Carlisle every reference to the moral and spiritual truths taught in God's Word and you have stripped them of their beauty and robbed them of their fragrance. Take down from off the walls of our best art galleries those pictures which portray scenes and incidents in the history of Israel and the life of our Lord and you have removed the richest gems from the crown of human genius. Remove from our statute-books every law which was founded upon the ethical conceptions of the Bible and you have annihilated the greatest factor in modern civilization. Rob our libraries of every book which is devoted to the work of elaborating and disseminating the precepts and concepts of Holy Writ and you have taken from us that which cannot be valued in dollars and cents.

" . . . Some one has said, 'Draw a line around the nations which have the Bible and you will then have divided between barbarism and civilization, between thrift and poverty, between selfishness and charity, between oppression and freedom, between life and the shadow of death.'"

(E. H. Bancroft, *Christian Theology*. Grand Rapids: Zondervan, 1961, p. 34) Used by permission.

PROJECT: As you study English or American Literature with your class, compile a list of Biblical quotations or expressions. Using a concordance find the reference and the setting for the original use of each one. Watch also for Biblical expressions in everyday usage.

## 7. Man's writings reflect his inner thoughts and desires; therefore we study literature to understand people.

This fact is implied by numerous statements in Scripture; for example:

Proverbs 16:23

*The heart of the wise teacheth his mouth and addeth learning to his lips.*

18:4

> The words of a man's mouth are as deep waters, and the wellspring of wisdom as a flowing brook.

Matthew 12:34-37

> Jesus speaking to the Pharisees: *34 O generation of vipers, how can ye, being evil, speak good things? For out of the abundance of the heart the mouth speaketh.*

*35 A good man out of the good treasure of his heart bringeth forth good things: and an evil man out of the treasure of the heart bringeth forth evil things . . . .*

15:18-20

> *18 But those things which proceed out of the mouth come forth from the heart . . . 20 These are the things which defile a man . . . .*

## 8. Our minds must be constantly filled with that which is pure and wholesome. We are responsible for those things with which we fill our minds.

Deuteronomy 17:18-20

> God's direction to Israel's future king: *18 . . . He shall write him a copy of this law in a book . . . 19 And it shall be with him, and he shall read therein all the days of his life: that he may learn to fear the Lord his God. to keep all the words of this law . . . 20 That his heart be not lifted up above his brethren, and that he turn not aside . . . .*

Psalm 1:1-3

> *1 Blessed is the man that walketh not in the counsel of*

*the ungodly . . . 2 But his delight is in the law of the Lord, and in his law doth he meditate day and night. 3 And he shall be like a tree planted . . . that bringeth forth fruit . . . whatsoever he doeth shall prosper.*

Philippians 4:8

> *Finally, brethren, whatsoever things are true, whatsoever things are honest, whatsoever things are just, whatsoever things are lovely, whatsoever things are of good report; if there be any virtue, and if there be any praise, think on these things.*

## 9. Not all literature is good. Some should be avoided entirely - even burned; other should be read with careful discernment.

Acts 19:18-20

> The example of new believers in Ephesus: *18 And many that believed came, and confessed, and shewed their deeds. 19 Many of them also which used curious arts brought their books together and burned them before all men: and they counted the price of them, and found it fifty thousand pieces of selver. 20 So mightily grew the word of God and prevailed.*

Proverbs 19:27

> Solomon's warning: *Cease, my son, to hear the instruction that causeth thee to err from the words of knowledge.*

Jeremiah 10:2

> *Thus saith the Lord, Learn not the way of the heathen...*

Colossians 2:8

> *Beware lest any man spoil you through philosophy and vain deceit, after the traditions of men, after the rudiments of the world, and not after Christ.*

1 Timothy 1:4

> Paul's instruction to young Pastor Timothy: *4 Neither give heed to fables and endless genealogies, which minister questions, rather than godly edifying . . . .*

4:7

> *But refuse profane and old wives' fables, and exercise thyself rather unto godliness.*

## 10. Knowledge of non-Christian literature may be used by God in His service.

Some examples:

Acts 7:22

> Stephen's testimony concerning Moses. *Moses was learned in all the wisdom of the Egyptians, and was mighty in words and in deeds.* [40 years of Egyptian learning and service]

Daniel 1:4, 17

> Daniel and his friends were chosen for special instruction in *"the learning and the tongue of the Chaldeans"* (v. 4); *"God gave them knowledge and skill in all learning and wisdom . . .* (v. 17).

Acts 22:3

Paul was brought up in Jerusalem at the feet of Gamaliel, an outstanding Jewish teacher, *"according to the perfect manner of the law of the fathers . . ."* - and this in spite of the fact that he was to be the apostle of Christ to the Gentiles primarily. Also 26:4, 5.

17:28

Paul was also familiar with Greek poetry and quoted from it in his message on Mars Hill to a Greek audience.

## QUOTES TO QUOTE

**TAKE AND READ. In 384 A. D. a young teacher from North Africa went to Milan, Italy, to take a position as teacher of rhetoric. While there, he became most troubled about his sins and sought desperately to get right with God. One day in the backyard of his home, while on the verge of almost complete despair, he heard the voice of a child next door chanting, "Take and read, take and read." Immediately he took his Bible and found that Jesus Christ was the way of complete forgiveness of sins. Through reading the Word of God this man's life was changed and he became St. Augustine, bishop of Hippo, one of the great Christians of all time.**

**-- Source unknown**

**MAN ON HIS KNEES. In the early days of the Republic, a stranger once asked at Congress how he could distinguish Washington. He was told, "You can easily distinguish him when Congress goes to prayer. Washington is the gentleman who kneels."**

**-- Author unknown**

## IDEAS TO TRY

In studying *Hamlet*, find Scriptural quotations or allusions. Discuss the ways in which they are used, both correctly and incorrectly. Help students to recognize the fact that the use of Bible expressions does not necessarily imply agreement with the Bible.

Compare an unabridged edition of *Pilgrim's Progress* with a children's edition, looking for ways in which the more difficult concepts are simplified. Use this study to show how important knowledge of readership is.

Compare a secular edition of Defoe's *Robinson Crusoe* with one from Moody Press, which contains passages from the original which deal with spiritual topics and which have been deleted from popular secular editions. Help students recognize the importance of the right editor and publisher; also the need to be aware of the possibility of more than one edition of a book.

Compare *Paradise Lost* with Genesis, chapters 1-3, noting the differences in the passages on the Creation, the Fall, etc. Show Biblical influence, but deviation as well. We must learn truth from the Bible.

Read several fables such as "The Fox and the Grapes," "The Hare and the Tortoise," "The Boy Who Cried Wolf." Compare the moral principles taught with some of those taught by familiar Bible stories.

After studying a poem which portrays a viewpoint that is not Biblical, encourage pupils to write one about the same topic, and perhaps in the same style, but expressing the Biblical view.

# 5

## Speech

God has much to say about speech; therefore this chapter is divided into several sections:

    I. The ability to speak
   II. The significance of speech
  III. Speaking for God
  IV. The content of our speech: what we say
   V. The manner of speech: how we speak
  VI. God's speaking

Because so much of Scripture is relevant to speech and many passages may be used as background for several concepts, an attempt has been made to place each one where it seems most useful.

## CONCEPT SUMMARY

I. Concerning the ability to speak

1. The ability to speak is given us by God.
2. God controls man's ability to speak and to be understood.
3. God will enable us to speak as we submit ourselves to Him.
4. God will guide even the choice of words and the organization of what we say, as we permit Him to do so.
5. God will direct us what to say when we have no opportunity to prepare.
6. God will answer prayer about our speaking, opening doors, making us bold for Him, controlling our tongues.

II. Concerning the significance of speech

1. Ability to speak differentiates men from animals.
2. Speech has great potential for good or evil.
   a. Our speech can praise and magnify God.
   b. Our speech can express antagonism toward God and our determination to be independent of Him.
   c. Our speech can encourage, uplift and unite people.
   d. Our speech can cause or aggravate problems in the lives of others.
   e. Our ability to speak allows us to confer with one another in solving problems and giving counsel.
   f. Our ability to speak enables us to pray and to share in one another's prayers.

    g. Our ability to speak makes possible a preaching and teaching ministry.

  3. Our speech is an index of our inner attitudes and our spiritual maturity.

  4. Sins of speech are considered by God to be very serious.

  5. Sinful speech affects the speaker adversely.

III. Concerning speaking for God

  1. God directs specific persons to speak for Him in particular situations.

  2. Speaking for God often brings misunderstanding and even persecution.

  3. Speaking for God demands honesty; to speak falsely or to fail to speak is an offense against God.

  4. God commends those who faithfully speak for Him.

  5. God expects all who trust Him to be loyal to Him in their speech.

IV. Concerning the content of our speech: what we say

  1. We must avoid what God condemns or forbids.

    a. We must count as sin any speech which fails to recognize God for who He is, or which insults one placed in authority by Him.

    b. We must not seek to add emphasis by swearing by anyone or anything; to do so is sin.

    c. Our talk must not hurt other people.

    d. We must not create divisions among the people of God.

    e. Crude or immoral speech has no place in the Christian life.

    f. Murmuring, griping, complaining - these do not honor God.

    g. Bragging, boasting, praising ourselves - such speech is unbecoming to Christians and fails to recognize God as the source of what is good.

    h. Talking too much and without thought brings trouble.

    i. Judging others, or disputing with them about conduct not forbidden by God, is forbidden.

  2. We must engage in the kinds of speaking which God commands or encourages in His Word.

a. We should speak to exhort, encourage and help others.

b. We should speak to share with another God's goodness and greatness.

c. We should speak to teach and preach the Word.

d. We are commanded to speak to witness to unbelievers that they might believe and be saved.

e. We must be friendly in our speech.

f. We must speak in prayer to God, both alone and with others.

g. We must praise God with our voices.

3. Our speech must be clean and pure.

4. Our lives and speech must be consistent if we are to be believed by God or people.

5. We must take seriously what we tell God.

V. Concerning our manner of speech: how we speak and conduct ourselves

1. We must speak with authority, being sure of what we say.

a. We must follow the example of Christ.

b. We must think before we speak, not talking so much that we are careless about the truth.

c. We must know what we are talking about, and especially so when we attempt to teach others.

2. We must show concern for people.

3. We must speak appropriately, according to the situation and the persons involved.

4. We must speak clearly, both in enunciation and in explanation.

5. We must use variety when we speak.

6. We must conduct ourselves in an orderly fashion when we, along with others, are speaking.

a. One at a time, taking turns

b. In language that others can understand, or that is interpreted to them

c. In a way which edifies and helps people to learn

d. Recognizing the fact that God does not give the same gifts to everyone

e. Placing love above ability to speak

7. We must be responsible for what we say.

## VI. Concerning God's speaking
  1. **When God speaks, things happen.**
  2. **When God speaks, He keeps His word.**
  3. **When God speaks, we must pay attention.**
  4. **When God speaks, we cannot answer, but only submit.**

### IDEAS TO TRY

PRACTICE GIVING CREDIT. Ask each pupil to give a description of someone who has been a real friend, including if possible an incident showing his love. Provide an alternate assignment, so that one who feels he has no friend will not feel left out.

SHOW POTENTIAL IN ONE CONVERSATION. Study the story of the woman at the well in John 4:6-45, noting how one conversation changed her life as well the lives of others. Ask pupils to write an imaginary conversation between the waterpot and the well, or a soliloquy by either one, commenting on the event and its significance.

SEE SERIOUSNESS OF LYING. Study Bible incidents in which someone lied (e.g., Adam, Eve, Abram, Peter). Assign specific characters to pupils. Assign others as interviewers, asking each one why he lied, and what were the results. Discuss.

DEVELOP APPRECIATION FOR ABILITY TO SPEAK AND HEAR. After studying Bible verses which show God's control over our ability to speak and hear, conduct a brief direct praise time. Let each pupil express to God his appreciation for these gifts, citing something specific. For example: "Thank You, Father, that I can say 'I love You'." "Thank You for the privilege of hearing the birds sing." "Praise God that we can talk and share His Word together."

### QUOTES TO QUOTE

When a person begins to tell white lies, it isn't long before he becomes color-blind.

Only people who do things get criticized.

To think of a clever but cutting remark, and then not make it - that is a sign of nobility.

Never answer an angry word with an angry word. It's the second one that makes the quarrel.

You can't have a gossiping tongue unless you have gossiping ears.

A lot of trouble in this world is caused by combining a narrow mind with a wide mouth.

-Author unknown
Quoted in the *Christian Teacher*, March-April, 1974

---

## SCRIPTURAL BACKGROUND

---

### I. Concerning the ability to speak

**1. The ability to speak is given us by God. Man is created in the image of God; God is a communicating Being.**

Genesis 1:27

*So God created man in his own image, in the image of God created he him . . . .*

2:18-20

From the beginning man was able to speak intelligently.

*18 And the Lord God said, It is not good that the man should be alone; I will make him an help meet for him 19 . . . God formed every beast . . . and brought them unto Adam to see what he would call them: and whatsoever Adam called every living creature, that was the name thereof. 20 And Adam gave names to all . . . .*

**2. God controls man's ability to speak and to be understood.**

Genesis 11:1, 7, 9

At the Tower of Babel: *1 And the whole earth was of one language and of one speech. 6 And the Lord said . . . 7 Go to, let us go down, and there confound their language, that they may not understand one another's speech. 9 Therefore is the name of it called Babel; because the Lord did there confound the language of all the earth . . . .*

Luke 1:20, 64

Zacharias after hearing of the coming birth of a son, John the Baptist: *20 . . . thou shalt be dumb, and not able to speak, until the day that these things shall be performed, because thou believest not my words, which shall be fulfilled in their season . . . . 64 And his mouth was opened immediately, and his tongue loosed, and he spake, and praised God.*

Also Ezekiel 3:26, 27.

Matthew 9:32, 33; 12:22, 23; 15:30, 31; Mark 7:31-37

On several occasions Christ healed those who were unable to speak.

Acts 2:7, 8; 10:46; 19:6

Believers controlled by the Holy Spirit, spoke other languages so that people from many nations understood at the same time. *7 And they were all amazed and marvelled, saying one to another, Behold, are not all these which speak Galileans? 8 And how hear we every man in our own tongue, wherein we were born?* (In verses 9-11, sixteen nationalities are listed.)

Mark 16:17

Christ's promise concerning this God-given ability: *17 And these signs shall follow them that believe; In my name shall they cast out devils; they shall speak with new tongues.*

1 Corinthians 12:4-11

The gifts of ability to speak in other languages and to interpret those languages are distributed by the Holy Spirit as He wills. *4 Now there are diversities of gifts, but the same Spirit . . . 8 For to one is given by the Spirit the word of wisdom; . . . 10 to another, diverse kinds of tongues; to another the interpretation of tongues: 11 But all these worketh that one and the selfsame Spirit, dividing to every man severally as he*

*wills.* Also 12:28-30.

Isaiah 32:4

Speaking of the Kingdom Age: *4 . . . The tongue of stammerers shall be ready to speak plainly.*

Zephaniah 3:9

After God's judgment of the nations He will remove the confusion of languages begun at Babel. *9 For then will I turn to the people a pure language, that they may all call upon the name of the Lord, to serve him with one consent.*

## 3. God will enable us to speak as we submit ourselves to Him.

Exodus 4:10-12

*10 Moses said unto the Lord, O my Lord, I am not eloquent . . . but I am slow of speech, and of a slow tongue. 11 And the Lord said unto him, Who hath made man's mouth? . . . have not I the Lord? 12 Now therefore go, and I will be with thy mouth, and teach thee what thou shalt say.* Also v. 15.

Isaiah 50:4

Isaiah's testimony: *4 The Lord God hath given me the tongue of the learned, that I should know how to speak*

*a word in season to him that is weary; he wakeneth morning by morning, he wakeneth mine ear to hear as the learned.*

Jeremiah 1:4-9

God called Jeremiah, whose response was, *I cannot speak: for I am a child.* God rebuked him saying, *Whatsoever I command thee thou shalt speak,* and then, *Behold, I have put my words in thy mouth.* Also Ezekiel 3:8-11, 1 Corinthians 2:1-13.

## 4. God will guide even in the choice of words and the organization of what we say, as we permit Him to do so.

1 Corinthians 2:1-6

Paul's testimony: *1 And I . . . came not with excellency of speech or of wisdom . . . 3 . . . I was with you in weakness, and in fear, and in much trembling. 4 And my speech and my preaching was not with enticing words of man's wisdom, but in demonstration of the Spirit and of power.*

Jeremiah 1:9

God to Jeremiah: *9 . . . Behold, I have put my words in thy mouth.*

Psalm 19:14

The Psalmist's prayer: *14 Let the words of my mouth, and the meditation of my heart, be acceptable in thy sight, O Lord, my strength, and my redeemer.*

## 5. God will direct us in what to say when we have no opportunity to prepare.

Matthew 10:18-20

*18 And ye shall be brought before governors and kings for my sake . . . 19 But when they deliver you up, take no thought how or what ye shall speak: for it shall be*

*given you in that same hour what ye shall speak. 20 For it is not ye that speak, but the Spirit of your Father which speaketh in you.* Also Mark 13:11; Luke 12:11, 12.

## 6. God will answer prayer about our speaking, opening doors and making us bold for Him; also controlling our tongues.

Ephesians 6:18-20

*18 Praying always . . . 19 And for me that utterance may be given unto me, that I may open my mouth bold-*

*ly, to make known the mystery of the gospel, 20 For which I am an ambassador in bonds: that therein I may speak boldly, as I ought to speak.*

Colossians 4:2-4

*2 Continue in prayer, and watch in the same with thanksgiving; 3 Withal praying also for us, that God would open unto us a door of utterance, to speak the mystery of Christ, for which I am also in bonds: 4 That I may make it manifest, as I ought to speak.*

Psalm 141:3

The example of the Psalmist: *3 Set a watch, O Lord, before my mouth; keep the door of my lips.* Also Psalm 19:14.

## II. Concerning the significance of speech.

### 1. Ability to speak differentiates men from animals.

Genesis 2:18-20

Though Adam was in the garden with an abundance of animals, there was no one on his own level with whom he could communicate; therefore God made woman. *18 And the Lord God said, It is not good that the man should be alone; I will make him an help meet for him. . . . 20 And Adam gave names to all cattle, and to the fowl of the air, and to every beast of the field; but for Adam there was not found an help meet for him.* Also 21-25.

### 2. Speech has great potential for good or evil.

Proverbs 18:21

*. . . Death and life are in the power of the tongue . . . .*

20:15

*There is gold, and a multitude of rubies: but the lips of knowledge are a precious jewel.*

### a. Our speech can praise and magnify God.

Psalm 34:1

*I will bless the Lord at all times: his praise shall continually be in my mouth.*

50:23

*Whoso offereth praise glorifieth me . . . .*

77:12

*I will meditate also of all thy work, and talk of thy doings.*

145:5

*I will speak of the glorious honour of thy majesty, and of thy wondrous works.*

### b. Our speech can express antagonism toward God and our determination to be independent of Him.

Psalm 10:4, 6, 11

*4 The wicked, through the pride of his countenance, will not seek after God: God is not in all his thoughts. 6 He hath said in his heart, I shall not be moved: for I shall never be in adversity.* [Verses 7-10 list the resulting outward sins.] *11 He hath said in his heart, God hath forgotten: he hideth his face; he will never see it* [i.e., my actions].

14:1

*The fool hath said in his heart, There is no God . . .* Also 53:1.

Ezekiel 35:12-14

God to Edom: *12 And thou shalt know that I am the Lord, and that I have heard all thy blasphemies which thou hast spoken against the mountains of Israel . . . . 13 Thus with your mouth ye have boasted against me, and have multiplied your words against me: I have heard them. 14 Thus saith the Lord God; When the whole earth rejoiceth, I will make thee desolate.*

Malachi 3:13, 14

God to Israel after the return from captivity in Babylon: *13 Your words have been stout against me, saith the Lord. Yet ye say, What have we spoken so much against thee? 14 Ye have said, It is vain to serve God: and what profit is it that we have kept his ordinance, and that we have walked mournfully before the Lord of hosts?*

Romans 1:21

*Because that, when they knew God, they glorified him not as God, neither were thankful . . . .*

### c. Our speech can encourage, uplift and unite people.

Proverbs 11:11

*By the blessing of the upright the city is exalted: but it is overthrown by the mouth of the wicked.*

14:25

*A true witness delivereth souls: but a deceitful witness speaketh lies.*

15:1

*A soft answer turneth away wrath: but grievous words stir up anger.*

16:24

*Pleasant words are as an honeycomb, sweet to the soul and health to the bones.* Also 15:4.

25:11-13

*11 A word fitly spoken is like apples of gold in pictures* [or, a basket] *of silver. 12 As an earring of gold, and an ornament of fine gold, so is a wise reprover upon an obedient ear. 13 As the cold of snow in the time of harvest, so is a faithful messenger to them that send him: for he refresheth the soul of his masters.*

27:9

*Ointment and perfume rejoice the heart; so doth the sweetness of a man's friend by hearty counsel.*

Ephesians 4:14, 15

*14 That we henceforth be no more children . . . 15 But speaking the truth in love may grow up into him in all things, which is the head, even Christ.*

4:29

Our speech is to be *that which is good to the use of edifying, that it may minister grace unto the hearers.*

### d. Our speech can cause or aggravate problems in the lives of others.

Proverbs 11:9

*An hypocrite with his mouth destroyeth his neighbor . . . .*

12:18

*There is that speaketh like the piercings of a sword . . . .*

16:28 (NASB)

*A perverse man spreads strife, and a slanderer separates intimate friends.*

18:8

*The words of a talebearer are as wounds, and they go down into the innermost parts of his belly.*

25:18

*A man that beareth false witness against his neighbour is a maul, and a sword, and a sharp arrow.*

Jeremiah 9:2-8

A description of the harm done by speech: *3 And they bend their tongues like their bow for lies: but they are not valiant for the truth . . . they proceed from evil to evil, and they know not me, saith the Lord. 4 Take heed every one of his neighbour, and trust ye not in any brother: for every brother will utterly supplant* [or, deal craftily], *and every neighbour will walk with slanders. 5 And they will deceive . . . and will not speak the truth . . . through deceit they refuse to know me, saith the Lord.*

Also Proverbs 26:22-28 and James 3.

### e. Our ability to speak allows us to confer with one another in solving problems and giving counsel.

Proverbs 11:14

*Where no counsel is, the people fall: but in the multitude of counsellors there is safety.*

24:6

*For by wise counsel thou shalt make thy war: and in the multitude of counsellors there is safety.*

27:5, 6

*5 Open rebuke is better than secret love. 6 Faithful are the wounds of a friend . . . .* Also 28:23.

Matthew 5:25, 26

*25 Agree with thine adversary quickly, whiles thou art in the way with him . . . .* [i.e., by resolving your problem promptly, you save considerable trouble.]

18:15-17

*15 Moreover if thy brother shall trespass against thee, go and tell him his fault between thee and him alone: if he shall hear thee, thou hast gained thy brother. 16 But if he will not hear thee, then take with thee one or two more, that in the mouth of two or three witnesses every word may be established. 17 And if he neglect to hear them, tell it unto the church: but if he neglect to hear the church, let him be unto thee as an heathen man and a publican.*

Acts 15:1-33

A church problem solved by counsel together.

### f. Our ability to speak enables us to pray and to share in one another's prayers.

Acts 1:14

A ten-day prayer meeting before the Day of Pentecost and the coming of the Holy Spirit. They were waiting as Christ had commanded them (v. 4).

12:5

*Peter therefore was kept in prison: but prayer was made without ceasing of the church unto God for him.*

14:23

*And when they [Paul and Barnabas] had ordained them elders in every church, and had prayed with fasting, they commended them to the Lord, on whom they believed.*

### g. Our ability to speak makes possible a preaching and teaching ministry.

Exodus 4:15, 16

God speaking to Moses about His using him and Aaron: *15 And thou shalt speak unto him, and put words in his mouth: and I will be with thy mouth, and with his mouth, and will teach you what ye shall do. 16 And he shall be thy spokesman unto the people: and he shall be, even he shall be to thee instead of God . . . .*

Nehemiah 8:2-8

After the rebuilding of the wall of Jerusalem: *2 And Ezra the priest brought the law before the congregation . . . . 5 And Ezra opened the book in the sight of all the people . . . . 7 Also Jeshua . . . and the Levites, caused the people to understand the law: and the people stood in their place. 8 So they read in the book in the law of God distinctly, and gave the sense, and caused them to understand the reading.*

Matthew 28:19, 20

*19 Go ye therefore, and teach all nations, baptizing . . . 20 Teaching them to observe all things whatsoever I have commanded you . . . .*

1 Timothy 4:13

Paul to young Pastor Timothy: (NASB) *Until I come, give attention to the public reading of the Scripture, to exhortation and teaching.*

### 3. Our speech is an index of our inner attitudes and our spiritual maturity.

Proverbs 10:18-21

One's lips reveal hatred or foolishness, wisdom or justice.

16:23

*The heart of the wise teacheth his mouth, and addeth learning to his lips.*

17:7

*Excellent speech becometh not a fool: much less do lying lips a prince.*

18:4

*The words of a man's mouth are as deep waters, and the wellspring of wisdom as a flowing brook.*

31:26

[A virtuous woman]*she openeth her mouth with wisdom; and in her tongue is the law of kindness.*

*Ecclesiastes 10:12, 13*

*12 The words of a wise man's mouth are gracious; but the lips of a fool will swallow up himself. 13 The beginning of the words of his mouth is foolishness: and the end of his talk is mischievous madness.*

Matthew 12:34, 35

*. . . Out of the abundance of the heart the mouth speaketh. 35 A good man out of the goodness of his heart bringeth forth good things: and an evil man out of the evil treasure bringeth forth evil things.* Also Luke 6:45.

15:18-20

*18 But those things which proceed out of the mouth come forth from the heart; and they defile the man. 19 For out of the heart proceed evil thoughts, murders, adulteries, fornications, thefts, false witness, blasphemies: 20 These are the things which defile a man . . . .*

James 1:26

Careless speech may indicate an empty life and an empty religion. *26 If any man among you seem to be religious, and bridleth not his tongue, but deceiveth his own heart, this man's religion is vain* [or empty].

3:2-6, 14-18

*2 For in many things we offend all. If any man offend not in word, the same is a perfect* [or mature] *man, and able also to bridle the whole body.*

Also Psalm 39:1-4; Proverbs 12:17, 18.

## 4. Sins of speech are considered by God to be very serious.

Psalm 34:13

David's warning: *Keep thy tongue from evil, and thy lips from speaking guile.*

39:1

David's testimony and concern: *I said, I will take heed to my ways, that I sin not with my tongue: I will keep my mouth with a bridle, while the wicked is before me.*

64:1-10

David prays that God will keep him from the evil devised by the wicked as they counsel together; he then reminds himself that God will judge them and will reward those who trust Him.

Proverbs 10:31, 32  (NASB)

*31 The mouth of the righteous flows with wisdom, but the perverted tongue shall be cut out. 32 The lips of the righteous bring forth what is acceptable, But the mouth of the wicked, what is perverted.*

13:3

*He that keepeth his mouth keepeth his life: but he that openeth wide his lips shall have destruction.*

Also Proverbs 19:5, 9, 19.

Isaiah 3:8

Talk against God is a basis for the ruin of a people. *8 For Jerusalem is ruined and Judah is fallen: because their tongue and their doings are against the Lord, to provoke the eyes of his glory.*

6:5

Isaiah's reaction to seeing the holiness of God: *5 . . . Woe is me! for I am undone; because I am a man of unclean lips, and I dwell in the midst of a people of unclean lips . . . .*

Jeremiah 34:8-22

King Zedekiah convenanted with the people of Jerusalem to free their servants; the people agreed and freed them (v. 10), but then demanded their return. God judged them for failure to mean what they said (15-17).

Matthew 12:36, 37

Jesus speaking: *36 But I say unto you, That every idle word that men shall speak, they shall give account thereof in the day of judgment. 37 For by thy words thou shalt be condemned.*

James 3:3-9

*3 Behold, we put bits in the horses' mouths, that they may obey us: and we turn about their whole body.*
*4 Behold also the ships, which though they be so great, and are driven of fierce winds, yet are they turned about with a very small helm, whithersoever the governor listeth.*
*5 Even so the tongue is a little member, and boasteth great things. Behold, how great a matter a little fire kindleth!*
*6 And the tongue is a fire, a world of iniquity: so is the tongue among our members, that it defileth the whole body, and setteth on fire the course of nature; and is set on fire of hell.*
*7 For every kind of beasts, and of birds, and of serpents, and of things in the sea, is tamed, and hath been tamed of mankind:*
*8 But the tongue can no man tame; it is an unruly evil, full of deadly poison.*
*9 Therewith bless we God, even the Father; and therewith curse we men, which are made after the similitude of God.*

## 5. Sinful speech affects the speaker adversely.

Proverbs 12:13

*The wicked is snared by the transgression of his lips: but the just shall come out of trouble.*

13:3

*. . . He that openeth wide his lips shall have destruction* [or ruin].

18:6, 7

*A fool's lips enter into contention, and his mouth calleth for strokes* [or, blows].     *7 A fool's mouth is his destruction, and his lips are the snare of his soul.*

21:23, 28

*23 Whoso keepeth his mouth and his tongue keepeth*

his soul from troubles. *28 A false witness shall perish . . . .*

26:22-28

These verses show the effects of tale-bearing on the inner life of a person (22-25, on his credibility to those who hear him (25), and on the whole congregation (26).

James 3:6 (NASB)

*And the tongue is a fire, the very world of iniquity; the tongue is set among our members as that which defiles the entire body, and sets on fire the course of our life, and is set on fire by hell.*

## III. Concerning speaking for God

### 1. God directs specific persons to speak for Him in particular situations.

Examples:

Exodus 3:1 through 4:18

God calls Moses: *3:10 Come now therefore, and I will send thee unto Pharaoh, that thou mayest bring forth my people the children of Israel out of Egypt.*

Joshua 4:1-10

God speaks to Joshua, and he to the people about making the two piles of stones as memorials to the crossing of Jordan.

6:2-21

God uses Joshua to instruct Israel in how they are to take Jericho as they march and blow trumpets and shout.

24:1-28

God uses Joshua to review the history of Israel and remind the people of His faithfulness, and their need of being true to Him.

1 Samuel 2:27-36

God sends a man of God to Eli to warn him of coming judgment because of his and his sons' disobedience.

8:7-18

God commands Samuel, now an old man, to warn the people what it will be like to have a king, and to promise that they may have one if they insist.

15:1-3

God sends Samuel to King Saul with directions to destroy completely the Amalekites, who had earlier defeated them (Num. 14:45).

Jeremiah 1:7, 16, 17

God speaking to Jeremiah: *7 . . . Whatsoever I command thee thou shalt speak. 16 And I will utter my judgments . . . 17 Thou therefore gird up thy loins, and arise, and speak unto them all that I command thee . . . .*

Also Jeremiah 2:1, 2; 7:1-4; 18:11; 19:1, 2, 11; 21:3, 4, 8; 22:1, 2; 26:1, 2, 7, 8, 12, 15 and many others which show how conscious Jeremiah was of God's directing him to be His spokesman.

PROJECT: Choose several Bible characters to whom God spoke frequently giving them messages to deliver for Him. Study through their lives, taking note of the times God directed them to speak in particular situations. You may wish to have each student choose one person, presenting his findings in chart form. Here are possible headings: PERSON, OCCASION, SUMMARY OF MESSAGE, RESULT OR RESPONSE. Some good subjects are: Moses, Joshua, Samuel, Elijah, Elisha, Jeremiah, the Minor Prophets, Paul the Apostle.

### 2. Speaking for God often brings misunderstanding and even persecution.

Examples:

Numbers 12:1-16

Miriam and Aaron speaking against Moses: *2 And they said, Hath the Lord indeed spoken only by Moses? hath he not spoken also by us? And the Lord heard it.* Though verse 1 indicates the fact that Aaron and Miriam were unhappy with Moses' Ethiopian wife, the issue God deals with is the question of who is His spokesman.

14:2-10

Moses and Aaron, who were God's spokesmen, along with Joshua and Caleb, the two spies who urged the people to trust God and move ahead, were so unpopular at times that "all the congregation bade stone them with stones" (v. 10).

16:1-3

Korah and 250 others under his leadership rebelled against Moses and Aaron's God-appointed leadership, saying, *3 . . . Ye take too much upon you, seeing all the congregation are holy, every one of them, and the Lord is among them: wherefore then lift ye up yourselves above the congregation of the Lord?*

Isaiah 6:8, 9

Sometimes God even tells His messenger that people will not understand or heed his message, yet He sends the messenger in spite of this expectation. God speaks to Isaiah: *9 And he said, Go, and tell this people, Hear ye indeed, but understand not; and see ye indeed, but perceive not.*

Jeremiah 20:1, 2, 7-10

*1 Now Pashur . . . chief governor in the house of the Lord heard that Jeremiah prophesied these things. 2 Then Pashur smote Jeremiah . . . and put him in the stocks . . . by the house of the Lord . . . .* [Jeremiah cries to the Lord] *7 O Lord, thou hast deceived me . . . I am in derision daily, every one mocketh me. 8 . . . the word of the Lord was made a reproach unto me, and a derision daily.* Also v. 14-18.

26:8-11, 24

Jeremiah was again harrassed and threatened, though God spared him from death.

26:20-23

Urijah, a prophet of God, is put to death because he prophesied the destruction of Jerusalem, repeating the message of Jeremiah.

See also Jeremiah 37:13-21; 38:1-13; and the footnote on page 814 of the Scofield Reference Bible for a summary of Jeremiah's prison experiences.

Jeremiah 43:2

The leaders of Judah, those left after most had been taken captive to Babylon, speaking to Jeremiah, displaying a somewhat typical attitude: *2 Then spake Azariah . . . and all the proud men, saying unto Jeremiah, Thou speakest falsely: the Lord our God hath not sent thee . . . .*

44:16, 17

The multitude speaking to Jeremiah: *16 As for the word that thou hast spoken unto us in the name of the Lord, we will not hearken unto thee. 17 But we will certainly do whatsoever thing goeth forth out of our own mouth . . . as we have done . . . for then had we plenty of victuals, and were well, and saw no evil.*

Ezekiel 2:3-5

God speaking to Ezekiel: *3 . . . I send thee to the children of Israel, to a rebellious nation that hath rebelled against me . . . . 4 For they are impudent children and stiffhearted . . . 5 And they, whether they will hear, or whether they will forbear . . . yet shall know there has been a prophet among them.*

Acts 4:1-7, 18

Peter's sermon after the healing of the lame man at the temple gate resulted in attack by the priests, the Sadducees and the ruler of the temple.

6:8-15

*8 And Stephen, full of faith and power, did great wonders . . . 9 Then there arose certain of the synagogue . . . disputing with Stephen . . . 12 And they stirred up the people . . . and came upon him and caught him, and brought him to the council, 13 And set up false witnesses . . . .*

Also 7:59 *And they stoned Stephen, calling upon God, and saying, Lord Jesus, receive my spirit.*

12:1-4

Peter imprisoned

PROJECT: In the Book of Acts, trace persecution of those who spoke for God. You may wish to record your findings in chart form: Who spoke? Who persecuted? What was the issue?

## 3. Speaking for God demands honesty; to speak falsely or to fail to speak is a serious offense.

Jeremiah 20:9

Jeremiah's testimony after suffering persecution: *9 Then said I, I will not make mention of him, nor speak any more in his name. But his word was in my heart as a burning fire shut up in my bones, and I was weary with forbearing, and I could not stay.*

23:16-32

God's judgment upon prophets who pretend to have God's message but speak something else: *28 The prophet that hath a dream, let him tell a dream; and he that hath my word, let him speak my word faithfully. What is the chaff to the wheat? saith the Lord. 29 Is not my word like as a fire? saith the Lord; and like a hammer that breaketh the rock in pieces? 30 There-fore, behold, I am against the prophets, saith the Lord, that steal my words every one from his neighbour. 31 Behold I am against the prophets, saith the Lord, that use their tongues, and say, He saith.*

26:2

*Thus saith the Lord . . . speak . . . all the words that I command thee to speak unto them; diminish not a word.*

28:1-17

Hananiah, a false prophet, contradicted the message that God had spoken through Jeremiah in Chapter 27. Jeremiah, at God's direction, pointed out his sin and pronounced his coming death within the year because he had *taught rebellion against the Lord* (v. 16).

29:21-23

*Thus saith the Lord of hosts . . . of Ahab . . . and of Zedekiah . . . which prophesy a lie unto you in my name. Behold I will deliver them into the hand of Nebuchadnezzar . . . 23 Because they have committed villany in Israel, and have committed adultery with their neighbors' wives, and have spoken lying words in my name, which I have not commanded them . . . .*

42:4

Jeremiah's promise to the Jewish leaders left in the land after the captivity: *4 Then Jeremiah the prophet said, . . . I will pray . . . whatsoever thing the Lord shall answer you, I will declare it unto you: I will keep back nothing from you.*

Ezekiel 2:1 through 3:21. See especially 2:3-5, 7, 8; 3:7, 18-21. Also 13:3, 6, 17; 33:7-9.

Acts 20:26, 27

Paul's testimony: *26 Wherefore I take you to record this day, that I am pure from the blood of all men. 27 For I have not shunned to declare unto you all the counsel of God.*

2 Corinthians 4:2

Paul's testimony that he had *renounced the hidden things of dishonesty, not walking in craftiness, nor handling the word of God deceitfully . . . .*

Galatians 1:6-12

Paul's concern because the Gospel message was being distorted: *9 . . . If any man preach any other gospel than that ye have received, let him be accursed . . . . 11 But I certify you, brethren, that the gospel which was preached of me is not after men. 12 For I neither received it of man, neither was I taught it, but by the revelation of Jesus Christ.*

1 Peter 4:11

*If any man speak, let him speak as the oracles of God.*

Revelation 22:18, 19

*18 For I testify unto every man that heareth the words of the prophecy of this book, If any man shall add unto these things, God shall add unto him the plagues that are written in this book: 19 And if any man shall take away from the words of the book of this prophecy, God shall take away his part out of the book of life, and out of the holy city, and from the things which are written in this book.*

## 4. God commends those who speak faithfully for Him.

Some examples:

Nehemiah 8, and 9:1-3

God records in great detail the faithful reading of the Word and the effects of that reading on the people who had returned from Babylon and rebuilt the wall of Jerusalem.

Jeremiah 38:7-13; 39:15-18

Ebedmelech spoke up to the king in Jeremiah's behalf (v. 8, 9); the king granted him thirty men to help in protecting Jeremiah, removing him from the miry dungeon (v. 10). God gave special word of assurance and protection to Ebedmelech for his action (39:15-18).

Ezekiel 9:3-6

This is part of Ezekiel's vision of the destruction that had taken place in Jerusalem and which he is reporting to the house of Israel, now in Babylon. *4 And the Lord said unto him* [i.e., the man with the writer's inkhorn], *Go . . . through the midst of Jerusalem, and set a mark upon the foreheads of the men that sigh and that cry for all the abominations that be done in the midst thereof. 5 And to the others he said in my hearing, Go ye after him through the city, and smite . . . 6 Slay utterly old and young . . . but come not near any man upon whom is the mark . . . .*

Luke 10:16

Jesus speaking to the seventy: *16 He that heareth you heareth me; and he that despiseth you despiseth me; and he that despiseth me despiseth him that sent me.*

Hebrews 11:20-22

God includes Isaac, Jacob and Joseph in this honor roll citing the fact that each one spoke of specific things yet future. They did it *by faith*, meaning that they spoke on the basis of what God had told them. See Genesis 27:27-29 (Isaac); 47:29-31 (Jacob); 50:24, 25 (Joseph).

2 Peter 2:5

God *saved Noah the eighth person, a preacher of righteousness, bringing in the flood upon the world of the ungodly.* See Genesis 6:8-22, where Noah's righteousness and his faithfulness in building the ark are described. In addition in this New Testament passage, God commends his speaking for Him.

Jude 14, 15

In Genesis 5:21-24 God testifies that Enoch *walked with God;* in Hebrews 11:5 He testifies further that Enoch *pleased God.* In neither report is any specific action described. Jude 14, 15 gives further detail indicating that, among other actions which pleased God, Enoch spoke.

*14 And Enoch also, the seventh from Adam, prophesied of these* [i.e., of the apostates described in the preceding and following verses] *saying, Behold, the Lord cometh with ten thousands of his saints, 15 To execute judgment upon all, and to convince all that are ungodly among them of all their ungodly deeds . . . and of all their hard speeches which ungodly sinners have spoken against him.*

## 5. God expects all who trust Him to be loyal to Him in their speech.

**Luke 12:8, 9**

*8 Also I say unto you, Whosoever shall confess me before men, him shall the Son of man confess before the angels of God; 9 But he that denieth me before men shall be denied before the angels of God.* Also Matthew 10:32, 33.

**John 12:42, 43**

*42 Nevertheless among the chief rulers also many believed on him; but because of the Pharisees they did not confess him, lest they should be put out of the synagogue: 43 For they loved the praise of men more than the praise of God.*

**Romans 10:9, 10**

*9 That if thou shalt confess with thy mouth the Lord Jesus, and shalt believe in thine heart that God hath raised him from the dead, thou shalt be saved. 10 For with the heart man believeth unto righteousness; and with the mouth confession is made unto salvation.*

**Hebrews 11:13-16**

*13 These all died in faith . . . and confessed that they were strangers and pilgrims on the earth. 14 For they that say such things declare plainly that they seek a country . . . . 16 But now they desire a better country, that is, an heavenly: wherefore God is not ashamed to be called their God: for he hath prepared for them a city.*

**1 John 4:15 and 2 John 7; also 1 John 4:2, 3**

These verses show that our confession of Christ is a test of the reality of our faith.

*15 Whosoever shall confess that Jesus is the Son of God, God dwelleth in him, and he in God.*

*7 For many deceivers are entered into the world, who confess not that Jesus Christ is come in the flesh. This is a deceiver and an antichrist.*

Also Ezekiel 3:18-21; 33:7, 8.

## IV. Concerning the content of our speech. God cares what we say.

### 1. We must avoid what God forbids or condemns.

#### a. We must recognize as sin any speech which fails to recognize God for who He is, or those given authority by Him.

**Exodus 20:7**

*Thou shalt not take the name of the Lord thy God in vain; for the Lord will not hold him guiltless that taketh his name in vain.* Also Deuteronomy 5:11.

**22:28**

*Thou shalt not revile the gods* [NASB: curse God] *nor curse the ruler of thy people.*

**Leviticus 24:15, 16**

*15 And thou shalt speak unto the children of Israel saying, Whosoever curseth his God shall bear his sin, 16 And he that blasphemeth the name of the Lord, he shall surely be put to death . . . as well the stranger, as he that is born in the land . . . .*

**Ecclesiastes 10:20**

*Curse not the king, no not in thy bedchamber: for a bird of the air shall carry the voice and that which hath wings shall tell the matter.*

**Isaiah 3:8**

Talk against the Lord is a basis for the ruin of a people. *8 For Jerusalem is ruined, and Judah is fallen: because their tongue and their doings are against the Lord, to provoke the eyes of his glory.*

**Jeremiah 44:15-17, 24-30**

An example of the seriousness of this sin.

*15 . . . A great multitude* [from Judah, now in Egypt, in disobedience to God] *. . . answered Jeremiah, saying, 16 As for the word that thou hast spoken unto us in the name of the Lord, we will not hearken unto thee. 17 But we will certainly do whatsoever thing goeth forth out of our own mouth . . . . 29* [God speaking] *And this shall be a sign unto you, saith the Lord, that I will punish you in this place, that ye may know that my words shall surely stand against you for evil.*

**Ezekiel 25:1-5**

*1 The word of the Lord came again unto me, saying,*

*2 Son of man, set thy face against the Ammonites and prophesy against them; 3 And say . . . Because thou saidst, Aha, against my sanctuary, when it was profaned; and against the land of Israel, when it was desolate; and against the house of Judah, when they went into captivity; 4 Behold, therefore I will deliver thee to the men of the east for a possession, and they shall set their palaces in thee, and make their dwellings in thee: they shall eat thy fruit, and they shall drink thy milk. 5 . . . and ye shall know that I am the Lord.*

Also verses 6-17. Note especially in verse 8 the emphasis on what Moab said that was offensive.

26:1-3.

Note again the sin of speech, which reveals attitude.

Daniel 5:1-5, 25-28, 30, 31

*1 Belshazzar the king made a great feast to a thousand of his lords . . . . 2 Belshazzar . . . commanded to bring the golden and silver vessels which his father Nebuchadnezzar had taken out of the temple which was in Jerusalem; that [they] might drink therein . . . . 4 They drank wine, and praised the gods of gold, and of silver, of brass, of iron, of wood, and of stone . . . .*

*26 God hath numbered thy kingdom and finished it . . . . 28 . . . Thy kingdom is divided and given to the Medes and Persians . . . . 30 In that night was Belshazzar the king of the Chaldeans slain. 31 And Darius the Median took the kingdom . . . .*

Acts 23:3-5

Paul recognized God's prohibition against cursing the high priest, even though his higher loyalty was now to Jesus Christ. Exodus 22:28.

Romans 2:21-24

*21 Because that, when they knew God they glorified him not as God, neither were thankful . . . 22 Professing themselves to be wise, they became fools, 23 And changed the glory of the uncorruptible God . . . 24 Wherefore God also gave them up to uncleanness through the lusts of their own hearts . . . .*

1 Corinthians 12:3

*Wherefore I give you to understand, that no man speaking by the Spirit of God calleth Jesus accursed; and that no man can say that Jesus is Lord, but by the Holy Ghost.*

### b. We must not seek to add emphasis by swearing by anyone or anything; to do so is sin.

Matthew 5:34-37

*34 But I say unto you, Swear not at all; neither by heaven; for it is God's throne: 35 Nor by the earth; for it is his footstool: neither by Jerusalem; for it is the city of the great King. 36 Neither shalt thou swear by thy head, because thou canst not make one hair white or black. 37 But let your communication be, Yea, Yea;*

*Nay, Nay: for whatsoever is more than these cometh of evil [or, of the evil one].*

James 5:12

*. . . Swear not, neither by heaven, neither by the earth, neither by any other oath: but let your yea be yea; and your nay, nay; lest ye fall into condemnation.*

### c. Our talk must not hurt other people; therefore we must refrain from cursing, slander, gossip, dishonesty, lying, mischief, flattery, teasing.

Exodus 20:16

*Thou shalt not bear false witness against thy neighbour.* Deuteronomy 5:20.

2 Kings 2:23, 24

Children were held accountable for teasing Elisha about his baldness. A gang of forty-two were killed by two female bears. (Note that in several of the more recent versions these "children" are called "young lads," or "young boys." They were not what we would commonly call "little children," though this term is used in KJ version.)

Psalm 10:7

God, in describing a wicked person, says: *His mouth is*

*full of cursing and deceit and fraud: under his tongue is mischief and vanity [emptiness].*

15:1-3

In describing one who shall abide in God's tabernacle, the Psalmist says: *3 He that backbiteth not with his tongue, nor doeth evil to his neighbour, nor taketh up a reproach against his neighbour.*

64:2-5

God describes as wicked those: *3 Who whet their tongue like a sword and bend their bows to shoot their arrows, even bitter words: 4 That they may shoot in secret at the perfect . . . . 5 They encourage themselves in the evil matter . . . they say, Who shall see them?*

140:3

Also a description of the wicked: *They have sharpened their tongues like a serpent; adders' poison is under their lips.* Also Romans 3:13.

Proverbs 4:24

*Put away from thee a froward* [or, deceitful] *mouth, and perverse* [or, devious] *lips far from thee.* Also 8:13.

6:16

*These six things doth the Lord hate: . . . 17 . . . a lying tongue . . . 19 A false witness that speaketh lies, and he that soweth discord among brethren.*

12:22

*Lying lips are abomination to the Lord: but they that deal truly are his delight.*

16:27

*An ungodly man diggeth up evil: and in his lips there is as a burning fire.* Also 11:13; 17:9; 18:8.

19:5-9

*A false witness shall not be unpunished, and he that speaketh lies shall not escape.*

26:18-28

Here are warnings against teasing, deceiving, gossip, contention, hatred, lying, flattery - all sins of speech. Note especially 18-20 as it relates to teasing:

*18 As a mad man who casteth firebrands, arrows, and death, 19 So is the man that deceiveth his neighbour, and saith, Am not I in sport? 20 Where no wood is, there the fire goeth out; so where there is no talebearer, the strife ceaseth.*

28:23

*He that rebuketh a man afterwards shall find more favor than he that flattereth with the tongue.*

29:5

*A man that flattereth his neighbour spreadeth a trap for his feet.*

Matthew 5:21, 22 (NASB)

*21 "You have heard that the ancients were told, 'You shall not commit murder' and 'Whoever commits murder shall be liable to the court.' 22 But I say to you that every one who is angry with his brother shall be guilty before the court; and whoever shall say to his brother, 'Raca,' shall be guilty before the supreme court; and whoever shall say, 'You fool,' shall be guilty enough to go into the hell of fire.*

2 Corinthians 12:20

*For I fear lest, when I come, I shall not find you such as I would . . . lest there be debates, envyings, wraths, strifes, backbitings, whisperings, swellings* [or, arrogance], *tumults.*

Ephesians 4:25

*Wherefore, putting away lying, speak every man truth with his neighbour: for we are members one of another.*

4:31

*Let all bitterness, and wrath, and anger, and clamour, and evil speaking* [or, slander], *be put away from you, with all malice.*

1 Peter 3:9, 10

*9 Not rendering evil for evil, or railing for railing* [or, insult for insult - NASB]; *but contrariwise blessing; knowing that ye are thereunto called, that ye should inherit a blessing. 10 For he that will love life, and see good days, let him refrain his tongue from evil, and his lips that they speak no guile.*

## d. We must not create divisions among the people of God.

Proverbs 6:16-19

*16 These six things doth the Lord hate: yea, seven are an abomination unto him: . . . 19 . . . and he that soweth discord among brethren.*

26:20, 21

*20 Where no wood is, there the fire goeth out: so where there is no talebearer, the strife ceases. 21 As coals are to burning coals, and wood to fire, so is a contentious man to kindle strife.*

Romans 16:17, 18

*17 . . . Mark them which cause divisions and offences contrary to the doctrine which ye have learned; and avoid them. 18 For they that are such serve not our Lord Jesus Christ . . . and by good words and fair speeches deceive the hearts of the simple.*

1 Corinthians 1:10-13

*10 I beseech you . . . that ye all speak the same thing, and that there be no divisions among you . . . .*

3:3

*For ye are yet carnal: for whereas there is among you envying, and strife, and divisions, are ye not carnal, and walk as men?*

Galatians 5:19-21 (NASB)

*19 Now the deeds of the flesh are evident, which are: . . . . 20 . . . enmities, strife, jealousy, outbursts of anger, disputes, dissensions, factions, 21 envyings . . . of which I forewarn you . . . that those who practice such things shall not inherit the kingdom of God.*

### e. Crude or immoral speech has no place in the Christian life.

Ephesians 4:29

*Let no corrupt* [unwholesome, or rotten] *communication proceed out of your mouth . . . .*

5:3, 4

*3 But fornication, and all uncleanness, or coveteousness, let it not be once named among you, as becometh saints; 4 Neither filthiness, nor foolish talking nor jesting, which are not convenient: but rather the giving of thanks.*

(NASB) *3 But do not let immorality or any impurity or greed even be named among you, as is proper among saints; 4 and there must be no filthiness and silly talk, or coarse jesting, which are not fitting, but rather giving of thanks.*

5:11, 12

*11 And have no fellowship with the unfruitful works of darkness, but rather reprove them. 12 For it is a shame even to speak of those things which are done of them in secret.*

### f. Murmuring, griping, complaining - these do not honor God.

Exodus 16:2-12

When Israel murmured against Moses and Aaron, complaining about their food (v. 2, 3), they were really murmuring against God. *8 And Moses said . . ., the Lord heareth your murmurings which ye murmur against him: and what are we? your murmurings are not against us, but against the Lord.* Also 17:2.

Numbers 14:1-37

God judges murmuring, considering it a serious sin. After the people complained against Moses and Aaron, and refused to follow the good report of Caleb and Joshua, God judged them with forty years of wandering in the desert, until all of that generation should die (v. 28-34).

The ten men who caused Israel to murmur and rebel were killed by a plague (36, 37).

16 :1-40

God judged Korah, Dathan, Abiram and the 250 others whom they led in complaining against the leadership of Moses. He opened up the earth for their whole families, and sent fire to kill the men themselves (v. 31-35).

16:41-50

The next day the crowd complained again, this time accusing Moses and Aaron of killing the two hundred fifty. God sent a plague that killed 14,700 persons (v. 49) before it was stopped by Aaron's making atonement for the sin of the congregation. See also Chapter 17, and 21:5-9.

1 Corinthians 10:10, 11

Paul, referring to Israel's experience in the wilderness wandering, says: *10 Neither murmur ye, as some of them also murmured and were destroyed of the destroyer. 11 Now all these things happened unto them for ensamples: and they were written for our admonition . . . .*

Philippians 2:14, 15

*14 Do all things without murmurings and disputings: 15 That ye may be blameless and harmless, the sons of God, without rebuke, in the midst of a crooked and perverse nation . . . .*

4:11

Paul's testimony as he thanked the Philippian church for their gifts: *11 Not that I speak in respect of want: for I have learned, in whatsoever state I am, therewith to be content.* Also v. 12.

1 Timothy 6:6-8

*6 But godliness with contentment is great gain. 7 For we brought nothing into the world, and it is certain we can carry nothing out. 8 And having food and raiment, let us be therewith content.*

Hebrews 13:5

*Let your conversation* [way of life] *be without covetousness; and be content with such things as ye have: for he hath said, I will never leave thee, nor forsake thee.*

Jude 16

Jude, in describing apostate teachers, says: *16 These are murmurers, complainers, walking after their own lusts . . . .*

### g. Bragging, boasting, praising ourselves - such speech is unbecoming to Christians and fails to recognize God as the source of what is good.

Psalm 12:3, 4

*3 The Lord shall cut off all flattering lips, and the tongue that speaketh proud things: 4 Who have said, With our tongue will we prevail; our lips are our own:*

*who is lord over us?*

Proverbs 27:2

*Let another man praise thee, and not thine own mouth; a stranger, and not thine own lips.*

Ezekiel 28:2-10

God speaking through Ezekiel to the king of Tyre: *2 . . . Because thine heart is lifted up, and thou hast said, I am a God, I sit in the seat of God, in the midst of the seas; yet thou art a man, and not God, though thou set thine heart as the heart of God . . . 6 Therefore thus saith the Lord God: Because thou hast set thine heart as the heart of God; 7 Behold I will bring strangers upon thee, the terrible of the nations; and they shall draw their swords against the beauty of thy wisdom. . . .*

29:3, 9

God condemns Egypt and her king, among other reasons, because as a nation she boasted that the Nile River was hers and that she had made it, failing to recognize God's place. *3 . . . Behold I am against thee, Pharaoh king of Egypt, . . . which said, My river is mine own, and I have made it myself. 9 And the land of Egypt shall be desolate and wasted; and they shall know that I am the Lord: because he hath said, The river is mine, and I have made it.*

35:12-14

God's judgment upon Edom (Mt. Seir) for boasting against Him.

Daniel 4:29-37

God's judgment of Nebuchadnezzar for his boasting: *30 The king spake and said, Is not this great Babylon, that I have built for the house of the kingdom by the might of my power, and for the honour of my majesty? 31 While the word was in the king's mouth, there fell a voice from heaven, saying, O king Nebuchadnezzar, to thee it is spoken; The kingdom is departed from thee. 32 And they shall drive thee from men, and thy dwelling shall be with the beasts . . . .*

Matthew 6:2, 5, 6

*2 Therefore when thou doest thine alms, do not sound a trumpet before thee, as the hypocrites do in the syna-gogues and in the streets, that they may have glory of men . . . . 5 And when thou prayest, thou shalt not be as the hypocrites are: for they love to pray standing in the synagogues and in the corners of the streets, that they may be seen of men. Verily I say unto you, They have their reward. 6 But thou, when thou prayest, enter into thy closet, and when thou hast shut thy door pray to thy Father which is in secret; and thy Father which seeth in secret shall reward thee openly.*

Matthew 26:33-35, 56

Peter's boasting brought him shame: *33 Peter answered and said unto him, Though all men shall be offended because of thee, yet will I never be offended . . . . 35 . . . Though I should die with thee, yet will I not deny thee. Likewise also said all the disciples. 56 . . . Then all the disciples forsook him and fled.*

Also 26:69-75.

1 Corinthians 4:7

*For who maketh thee to differ from another? and what hast thou that thou didst not receive? now if thou didst receive it, why dost thou glory, as if thou hadst not received it?*

2 Corinthians 10:17, 18

*17 But he that glorieth, let him glory in the Lord. 18 For not he that commendeth himself is approved, but whom the Lord commendeth.*

11:1-30

Paul is very hesitant to tell all that the Lord has done for him by way of special experiences, lest he be thought to boast. He recognizes the very real danger of self-exaltation:

*7 And lest I should be exalted above measure through the abundance of revelations, there was given to me a thorn in the flesh, the messenger of Satan to buffet me, lest I should be exalted beyond measure.*

Philippians 2:3

*Let nothing be done through strife or vainglory [empty conceit, in NASB]; but in lowliness of mind let each esteem the other better than themselves.*

## h. Talking too much and without thought brings trouble.

Proverbs 29:11

*A fool uttereth all his mind, but a wise man keepeth it in till afterwards.*

Ecclesiastes 5:2, 3

*2 Be not rash with thy mouth, and let not thine heart be hasty to utter anything before God: for God is in heaven and thou upon the earth: therefore let thy words be few. 3 . . . a fool's voice is known by multitude of words.* Also v. 4-7.

See also later section dealing with the manner of speech.

### i. Judging others, or disputing with them about conduct not forbidden by God, is forbidden.

Matthew 7:1-3

*1 Judge not, that ye be not judged. 2 For with what judgment ye judge, ye shall be judged: and with what measure ye mete, it shall be measured to you again. 3 And why beholdest thou the mote that is in thy brother's eye, but considerest not the beam that is in thine own eye? Also v. 4, 5; Luke 6:37.*

Romans 14:1-13

*1 Him that is weak in the faith receive ye, but not to doubtful disputations* [NASB: but not for the purpose of passing judgment on his opinions].
*2 For one believeth that he may eat all things: another who is weak, eateth herbs.*
*3 Let not him that eateth despise him that eateth not; and let not him which eateth not judge him that eateth: for God hath received him.*
*4 Who art thou that judgest another man's servant? to his own master he standeth or falleth. Yea, he shall be holden up: for God is able to make him stand.*
*5 One man esteemeth one day above another: another esteemeth every day alike. Let every man be fully persuaded in his own mind.*
*6 He that regardeth the day, regardeth it unto the Lord; and he that regardeth not the day, to the Lord he doth not regard it. He that eateth, eateth to the Lord, for he giveth God thanks; and he that eateth not, to the Lord he eateth not, and giveth God thanks.*
*10 But why dost thou judge thy brother? or why dost thou set at nought thy brother? for we shall all stand before the judgment seat of Christ.*
*12 So then every one of us shall give account of himself to God.*
*13 Let us not therefore judge one another any more: but judge this rather, that no man put a stumblingblock or an occasion to fall in his brother's way.*

1 Corinthians 8:8, 9

Concerning food that had been previously offered to idols: *8 But meat commendeth us not to God: for neither, if we eat, are we the better; neither, if we eat not, are we the worse. 9 But take heed lest by any means this liberty of yours become a stumblingblock to them that are weak.*

Colossians 2:16, 17

*16 Let no man therefore judge you in meat, or in drink, or in respect of an holyday, or of the new moon, or of the sabbath days: 17 Which are a shadow of things to come; but the body is of Christ. Also v. 18-23.*

James 4:11, 12

*11 Speak not evil of one another, brethren. He that speaketh evil of his brother, and judgeth his brother, speaketh evil of the law, and judgeth the law: but if thou judge the law, thou art not a doer of the law, but a judge. 12 There is one lawgiver, who is able to save and to destroy: who art thou that judgest another?*

Also Romans 2:1-3; 1 Corinthians 4:1-5.

## 2. We must engage in the kinds of speaking which God commands or encourages in His Word.

### a. We should speak to exhort, encourage and help others.

Proverbs 25:15, 25

*15 By long forbearing is a prince persuaded, and a soft tongue breaketh the bone. 25 As cold waters to a thirsty soul, so is good news from a far country.*

1 Corinthians 14:26

*. . . Let all things be done unto edifying.*

Ephesians 4:25, 29

*25 Wherefore putting away lying, speak every man truth with his neighbor: for we are members one of another. 29 Let no corrupt communication proceed out of your mouth, but that which is good to the use of edifying, that it may minister grace to the hearers.*

5:18, 19

*18 . . . Be filled with the Spirit; 19 Speaking to yourselves in psalms and hymns and spiritual songs, singing and making melody in your heart to the Lord.*

Hebrews 10:24, 25

*24 And let us consider one another to provoke unto love and to good works: 25 . . . exhorting one another: and so much the more, as ye see the day approaching.*

1 Timothy 5:1

*Rebuke not an elder, but intreat him as a father, and the younger men as brethren.* (Written by Paul to young Pastor Timothy)

### b. We should speak to share with one another God's goodness and greatness.

Psalm 77:12

*I will meditate also of all thy work, and talk of thy doings.*

145:4-7

*4 One generation shall praise thy works to another, and shall declare thy mighty acts. 5 I will speak of the glorious honour of thy majesty, and of thy wondrous works. 6 And men shall speak of the might of thy terrible acts: and I will declare thy greatness. 7 They shall abundantly utter the memory of thy great goodness, and shall sing of thy righteousness.*

145:10-12

*10 All thy works shall praise thee, O Lord; and thy saints shall bless thee. 11 They shall speak of the glory of thy kingdom, and talk of thy power; 12 To make known to the sons of men his mighty acts, and the glorious majesty of his kingdom.*

Malachi 3:16

*Then they that feared the Lord spake often one to another: and the Lord hearkened, and heard it, and a book of remembrance was written before him for them that feared the Lord and that thought upon his name.*

Acts 14:27

Paul and Barnabas, after returning from the first missionary journey: *27 And when they were come, and had gathered the church together, they rehearsed all that God had done with them and how he had opened the door of faith unto the Gentiles.*

Also Acts 2:46, 47.

### c. We should speak to teach and preach the Word.

Matthew 28:19, 20

*19 Go ye therefore, and teach all nations . . . 20 Teaching them to observe all things whatsoever I have commanded you . . . .*  Also Mark 16:15.

1 Timothy 4:13 (NASB)

Paul to Timothy, a young pastor: *13 Until I come, give attention to the public reading of the Scripture, to exhortation and teaching.*

2 Timothy 2:24, 25

*24 And the servant of the Lord must . . . be gentle unto all men, apt to teach, patient, 25  In meekness instructing those that oppose themselves, if God peradventure will give them repentance to the acknowledging of the truth.*

4:2

*Preach the word; be instant in season, out of season; reprove, rebuke, exhort will all longsuffering and doctrine.*

Also Deuteronomy 6:6, 7, 20-23; 11:19; Psalm 78:1-6.

### d. We are commanded to speak as witnesses to unbelievers that they might believe and be saved.

Romans 10:14, 17

*14 How then shall they call on him in whom they have not believed? and how shall they believe in him of whom they have not heard? and how shall they hear without a preacher? 17 So then faith cometh by hearing, and hearing by the word of God.*

1 Peter 3:15

*. . . And be ready always to give an answer to every man that asketh you a reason of the hope that is in you with meekness and fear.*

### e. We must be friendly in our speech.

Proverbs 18:24

*A man that hath friends must show himself friendly: and there is a friend that sticketh closer than a brother.*

22:11 (NASB)

*He who loves purity of heart and whose speech is gracious [or, has grace on his lips], the king is his friend.*

Matthew 5:44-47

*47 And if ye salute your brethren only, what do ye more than others? do not even the publicans so?*

PROJECT: The early Christians were careful to ask that their greetings be conveyed to others. Though the request was frequently a written one, the greeting was an oral one. Look up these instances where the writer asks that the reader greet a person or group: Romans 16:5-23; 1 Corinthians 16:19, 20; Philippians 4:21; Colossians 4:15, 16; 2 Timothy 4:19; Titus 3:15; Hebrews 13:24; 3 John 14.

Note also the many times when a writer, even when many important matters were to be said, made a point of sharing the greetings of others. Surely the example is one of friendliness and caring. See 2 Corinthains 13:13; Philippians 4: 21, 22; Colossians 4:10-12; 2 Timothy 4:21; Titus 3:15; Philemon 23; Hebrews 13:24; 1 Peter 5:13; 3 John 14.

## f.  We must speak in prayer to God, both alone and with others.

2 Chronicles 7:13, 14

God speaking to King Solomon after the dedication of the temple: *13 If I shut up heaven that there be no rain, or if I command the locusts to devour the land, or if I send pestilence among my people: 14 If my people, which are called by my name, shall humble themselves, and pray, and seek my face, and turn from their wicked ways; then will I hear from heaven, and will forgive their sin, and will heal their land.*

Psalm 5:3

The example of David, "a man after God's own heart": *3 My voice shalt thou hear in the morning, O Lord; in the morning will I direct my prayer unto thee, and will look up.*

55:16, 17

Again, David's testimony:  *16 As for me, I will call upon God; and the Lord shall save me. 17 Evening, and morning, and at noon will I pray, and cry aloud: and he shall hear my voice.*

Matthew 6:6

*But thou, when thou prayest, enter into thy closet, and when thou hast shut thy door, pray to thy Father which is in secret; and thy Father which seeth in secret shall reward thee openly.*

7:7, 8

*7 Ask, and it shall be given you; seek and ye shall find; knock and it shall be opened unto you. 8 For everyone that asketh receiveth . . . .*

18:19

*Again I say unto you, That if two of you agree on earth as touching any thing that they shall ask, it shall be done for them of my Father which is in heaven.*

Philippians 4:6

*Be careful [or, anxious] for nothing; but in everything by prayer and supplication with thanksgiving let your requests be made known unto God.*

1 Timothy 2:8

*I will therefore that men pray everywhere . . . .*

James 4:2

*. . . Ye have not because ye ask not.*

5:16

*Confess your faults one to another, and pray one for another, that ye may be healed. The effectual prayer of a righteous man availeth much.*

Also v. 17, 18, the example of Elijah.

## g.  We must praise God with our voices.

Psalm 50:23

*Whoso offereth praise glorifieth God . . . .*

34:1-3

David's testimony: *1 I will bless the Lord at all times: his praise shall continually be in my mouth. 2 My soul shall make her boast in the Lord: the humble shall hear thereof and be glad. 3 O magnify the Lord with me, and let us exalt his name together.*

105:1

*O give thanks unto the Lord; call upon his name: make known his deeds among the people.*

107:31, 32

*31 Oh that men would praise the Lord for his goodness,* *and for his wonderful works to the children of men! 32 Let them exalt him also in the congregation of the people, and praise him in the assembly of the elders.*

Isaiah 38:18, 19

Hezekiah speaking after God healed him: *18 For the grave cannot praise thee, death cannot celebrate thee; they that go down into the pit cannot hope for thy truth. 19 The living, the living, he shall praise thee, as I do this day: the father to the children shall make known thy truth.*

Acts 2:46, 47

The example of the church in Jerusalem: *47 And they continued daily with one accord in the temple and . . .*

from house to house . . . *47 Praising God, and having favour with all the people.*

**1 Corinthians 15:57**

Paul bursts into praise as he thinks about the coming Rapture of believers and their transformation: *57 But thanks be unto God, which giveth us the victory through our Lord Jesus Christ.*

Also similar bursts of praise in others of Paul's writings. See Romans 16:27; Ephesians 1:3, 20; Philippians 4:20; 1 Timothy 1:17. Look for similar expressions by Peter and Jude in their epistles.

PROJECT: Make a study of the Psalms, looking for all the reasons given for which we should praise God. Record each one; then categorize them.

PROJECT: In the Psalms the word *Selah* is often found. It means a pause with the thought: "Think of that!" As you study through the Psalms, note in each case what we are told to think about and in many cases praise God for. After making your list, classify the items.

## 3. Our speech must be clean and pure.  (See also Section IV, 1, pages 50-55.)

**Job 27:4-6**

Job's determination not to sin in speech, even under great difficulty. *4 My lips shall not speak wickedness, nor my tongue utter deceit. 5 God forbid that I should justify you: till I die I will not remove mine integrity from me. 6 My righteousness I hold fast, and will not let it go: My heart shall not reproach me so long as I live.*

**Psalm 15:1-3**

God's concern about who approaches Him: *1 Lord, who shall abide in thy tabernacle? who shall dwell in thy holy hill? . . . . 3 He that backbiteth not with his tongue, nor doeth evil to his neighbour, nor taketh up a reproach against his neighbour.*

**Proverbs 12:22**

*Lying lips are abomination to the Lord: but they that deal truly are his delight.*

**Titus 3:1, 2**

Spoken concerning the responsibilities of a pastor: *1 Put them in mind . . . 2 To speak evil of no man, to be no brawlers, but gentle, showing all meekness unto all men.*

Also Ephesians 4:29-32; James 4:11, and many other passages.

## 4. Our lives and speech must be consistent if we are to be believed by God or by people.

**1 Samuel 12:1-5**

Samuel a prophet of God, whose integrity was so carefully guarded that he dared to issue a challenge to Israel: *2 . . . I am old and grayheaded; and behold my sons are with you: and I have walked before you from my childhood unto this day. 3 Behold, here I am: witness against me before the Lord, and before his anointed: whose ox have I taken? or whose ass have I defrauded? whom have I oppressed? or of whose hand have I received any bribe to blind mine eyes therewith? and I will restore it you. 4 And they said, Thou hast not defrauded us . . . .*

**Psalm 50:16-23**

*16 But unto the wicked God saith, What hast thou to do to declare my statutes, or that thou shouldst take my covenant in thy mouth? 17 Seeing thou hatest instruction and casteth my words behind thee . . . .* [Details of their inconsistency are given in v. 18-21.]

**Proverbs 15:26**

*. . . The words of the pure are pleasant words.*

**28:13**

*He that covereth his sins shall not prosper: but whoso confesseth and forsaketh them shall have mercy.*

**John 8:46**

The life and actions of Christ were so pure that He could say without hesitation:  *46 Which of you convinceth me of sin?*

**Romans 2:17-23**

*21 Thou therefore which teachest another, teachest thou not thyself? thou that preachest a man should not steal, dost thou steal? 22 Thou that sayest a man should not commit adultery, dost thou commit adultery? thou that abhorrest idols, dost thou commit sacrilege? 23 Thou that makest thy boast of the law, through breaking the law dishonourest thou God?*

**Titus 2:6-8**

Paul encourages Titus to exhort young men (v. 6) to be *7 . . . a pattern of good works . . . sound [in] speech, that cannot be condemned; that he that is of the contrary part may be ashamed, having no evil thing to say of you.*

**Ephesians 5:4**

Paul, listing sins not consistent with the Christian life: *4 Neither filthiness, nor foolish talking, nor jesting, which is not convenient* [or, fitting]: *but rather giving of thanks.*

James 1:26

*If any man among you seem to be religious, and bridleth not his tongue, but deceiveth his own heart, this man's religion is vain.* See also James 3:9-13.

## 5. We must take seriously what we tell God.

Levitucus 5:4-6

Under the Law, one who made a rash vow, good or bad, and realized later that it was rash had responsibility to recognize his sin, confess it, and bring the proper offering to the Lord.

Numbers 30

*2 If a man vow a vow unto the Lord, or swear an oath to bind his soul with a bond; he shall not break his word, he shall do according to all that proceedeth out of his mouth.* [This again is under the Law for Israel, but expresses God's concern for what people say.]

3-16 Some exceptions were made for women when they were under the jurisdiction of their fathers or husbands.

1 Peter 3:15, 16

*15 . . . Be ready always to give an answer to every man that asketh you a reason of the hope that is in you . . . 16 Having a good conscience; that whereas they speak evil of you, as of evil doers, they may be ashamed that falsely accuse your good conversation* [or, behavior] *in Christ.*

Job 1:21, 22

In spite of the trials which came to Job, he was careful in what he said about God or to Him *2 In all this Job sinned not, nor charged God foolishly.*

Ecclesiastes 5:1-6

*1 Keep thy foot when thou goest to the house of God . . . . 2 Be not rash with thy mouth, and let not thine heart be hasty to utter any thing before God: for God is in heaven, and thou upon the earth: therefore let thy words be few. 4 When thou vowest a vow unto God, defer not to pay it; for he hath no pleasure in fools: pay that which thou hast vowed. 5 Better is it that thou shouldest not vow, than that thou shouldest vow and not pay.*

## V. Concerning the manner of speech: how we speak and conduct ourselves

## 1. We must speak with authority, being sure of what we say.

### a. We must follow the example of Christ, even as Paul did.

Matthew 7:28, 29

*28 And it came to pass, when Jesus had ended these sayings, the people were astonished at his doctrine: 29 For he taught them as one having authority, and not as the scribes.* Also Mark 1:22.

Acts 9:29

The Apostle Paul, soon after his conversion, is described: *29 And he spake boldly in the name of the Lord Jesus, and disputed among the Grecians: but they went about to slay him.*

19:8

*And he* [Paul] *went into the synagogue, and spake boldly for the space of three months, disputing and persuading the things concerning the kingdom of God.*

Ephesians 6:19, 20

Paul asks that they pray: *19 For me, that utterance*

*may be given unto me, that I may open my mouth boldly, to make known the mystery of the gospel, 20 For which I am an ambassador in bonds: that therein I may speak boldly, as I ought to speak.*

Note that he wanted this kind of bold speech, even though he was already in prison for the Gospel's sake.

2 Corinthians 3:12

*Seeing then that we have such hope, we use great plainness* [or, boldness, in NASB] *of speech.*

PROJECT: In the Book of Ezekiel, note how many times Ezekiel specifically says that it was the Lord who told him what to say. Do the same with Jeremiah. They were concerned that the Authority for their statements be recognized.

**"Never man spake like this Man!"**

### b. We must think before we speak, not talking so much that we are careless about the truth.

Proverbs 10:19

*In the multitude of words, there wanteth not sin: but he that refraineth his lips is wise.*

12:23

*A prudent man concealeth knowledge: but the heart of fools proclaimeth foolishness.*

16:23

*The heart of the wise teacheth his mouth, and addeth learning to his lips.*

15:2, 28

*2 The tongue of the wise useth knowledge aright: but the mouth of fools pours out foolishness.*
*28 The heart of the righteous studieth to answer: but the mouth of the wicked poureth out evil things.*

17:27, 28

*27 He that hath knowledge spareth his words: and a man of understanding is of an excellent spirit. 28 Even a fool, when he holdeth his peace, is counted wise: and he that shutteth his lips is esteemed a man of understanding.*

29:11, 20

*11 A fool uttereth all his mind: but a wise man keepeth it in till afterwards. 20 Seest thou a man that is hasty in his words? There is more hope of a fool than of him.*

Ecclesiastes 5:2, 3

*2 Be not rash with thy mouth . . . let thy words be few. 3 . . . a fool's voice is known by multitude of words.*

10:20 *A warning against careless private talk.*

*James 1:19*

Wherefore, my beloved brethren, let every man be swift to hear, slow to speak, slow to wrath.

### c. We must know what we are talking about, and especially so when we try to teach others.

Romans 12:6-8

The teacher is to give himself wholeheartedly to his teaching. *6 Having then gifts differing according to the grace that is given to us, whether prophecy, let us prophesy . . . 7 Or ministry, let us wait on our ministering: or he that teacheth, on teaching.*

1 Timothy 1:6, 7

Paul warns of those who seek to teach without having sound doctrine themselves: *6 From which [doctrine] some having swerved have turned aside unto vain jangling; 7 Desiring to be teachers of the law; understanding neither what they say, nor whereof they affirm.* Also Romans 2:21.

Jude 8-10

God condemns those who *. . . speak evil of those things which they know not . . . .*

## 2. We must show concern for people.

Proverbs 11:12, 13

*12 He that is void of wisdom despiseth his neighbor: but a man of understanding holdeth his peace. 13 A talebearer revealeth secrets: but he that is of a faithful spirit concealeth the matter.* See also NASB.

17:9

*He that covereth a transgression seeketh love; but he that repeateth a matter separateth very friends.*

Luke 18:16

The example of Christ: *16 But Jesus . . . said, Suffer little children to come unto me, and forbid them not: for of such is the kingdom of God.*

John 8:7

Jesus spoke to those ready to stone the immoral woman: *7 . . . He that is without sin among you, let him first cast a stone at her.*

Ephesians 4:32

*And be ye kind one to another, tenderhearted, forgiving one another, even as God for Christ's sake hath forgiven you.*

Colossians 4:6

*Let your speech be alway with grace . . . .*

James 1:17

*But the wisdom that is from above is first pure, then peaceable, gentle, easy to be intreated, full of mercy and good fruits, without partiality, and without hypocrisy.*

## 3. We must speak appropriately, according to the situation and the persons involved.

Proverbs 15:1

*A soft answer turneth away wrath . . . .*

25:11

*A word fitly spoken is like apples of gold in pictures of silver.*

(NASB) *Like apples of gold in settings of silver is a word spoken in right circumstances.*

25:15

*By long forbearing is a prince [or, ruler] persuaded, and a soft tongue breaketh the bone.*

26:5

*Answer a fool according to his folly, lest he be wise in his own conceit.*

(NASB) *Answer a fool as his folly deserves, lest he be wise in his own eyes.*

27:14

*He that blesseth his friend with a loud voice, rising early in the morning, it shall be counted a curse to him.*

29:9

*If a wise man contendeth with a foolish man, whether he rage or laugh, there is no rest.*

Ecclesiastes 3:1-7

*1 To everything there is a season, and a time to every purpose under heaven: . . . 7 . . . a time to keep silence and a time to speak.*

9:17

*The words of wise men are heard in quiet more than the cry of him that ruleth among fools.*

(NASB) *The words of the wise heard in quietness are better than the shouting of a ruler among fools.*

## 4. We must speak clearly, both in enunciation and in explanation.

Nehemiah 8:15-13

The example of Ezra in reading publicly the book of the Law: *5 And Ezra opened the book in the sight of all the people . . . . 7 Also Jeshua . . . [and others] caused the people to understand the law . . . . 8 So they read in the law of God distinctly, and gave the sense, and caused them to understand the reading . . . . 13 And on the second day were gathered together the chief of the fathers of all the people, the priests, and the Levites, unto Ezra the scribe, even to understand the words of the law.*

1 Corinthians 14:15-19

Paul expresses concern that he speak in a way that people will understand and learn: *15 . . . I will pray with the spirit and with the understanding also . . . . 16 Else . . . how shall . . . the unlearned say Amen at thy giving of thanks, seeing he understandeth not what thou sayest? . . . 19 . . . I had rather speak five words with my understanding, that by my voice I might teach others also than ten thousand words in an unknown tongue.*

14:33, 40

*33 For God is not the author of confusion, but of peace . . . . 40 Let all things be done decently and in order.*

## 5. We must use variety when we speak.

Matthew 5, 6, 7

Here in the Sermon on the Mount, note the variety of techniques the Lord uses as He speaks. Watch for imperative statements, questions, similes and metaphors, illustrations, summary statements, parables, poetic expressions, allusions to what He knows they accept (e.g., the Law), giving of a pattern (6:9-13), etc.

Matthew 24, 25

In the Olivet Discourse, note again the variety used.

PROJECT: Choose other longer discourses of Christ and study them for the variety in speech. For instance, study the conversation of Jesus and Nicodemus in John 3, or the interaction between Jesus and the Samaritan woman in John 4:6-29. In Matthew 18:1-10, He does some unusual things in answering the question, "Who is the greatest in the kingdom of heaven?"

## 6. We must conduct ourselves in an orderly fashion when we, along with others, are speaking.

1 Corinthians 14:33, 40

*33 For God is not the author of confusion, but of peace, as in all churches of the saints. 40 Let all things be done decently and in order.*

### a. One at a time, taking turns

1 Corinthians 14:29-31

*29 Let the prophets speak two or three, and let the other judge. 30 If anything be revealed to another that sitteth by, let the first hold his peace. 31 For ye may all prophesy one by one, that all may learn, and all may be comforted.*

### b. In language that others may understand, or that is interpreted to them

Though the emphasis in 1 Corinthians 14 is primarily on speaking in <u>languages</u> which others do not understand, application can also be made to the use of <u>vocabulary</u> which is understood by the hearers. A major thrust of the passages is on understanding by others, in order that they might learn and be edified.

1 Corinthians 14:9-11, 27, 28

*9 So likewise ye, except ye utter by the tongue words easy to be understood, how shall it be known what is spoken? for ye shall speak into the air. 10 There are, it may be, so many kinds of voices in the world, and none of them is without signification [or, meaning]. 11 Therefore if I know not the meaning of the voice [or, language], I shall be unto him that speaketh a barbarian, and he that speaketh shall be a barbarian unto me.*

*27 If any man speak in an unknown tongue, let it be by two, or at the most by three, and that by course; and let one interpret. 28 But if there be no interpreter, let him keep silence in the church; and let him speak to himself, and to God.*

### c. In a way which edifies and helps people to learn

1 Corinthians 14:5, 12, 15, 16, 17, 19, 23-26

*5 . . . for greater is he that prophesieth than he that speaketh in tongues, except he interpret, that the church may receive edifying. 12 Even so ye, forasmuch as ye are zealous of spiritual gifts, seek that ye may excel to the edifying of the church. 15 . . . I will pray with the spirit, and I will pray with the understanding also . . . 16 Else . . . how shall he that occupieth the room of the unlearned say Amen at thy giving of thanks, seeing he understandest not what thou sayest? 17 For thou verily givest thanks well, but the other is not edified. 19 Yet in the church I had rather speak five words with my understanding, that by my voice I might teach others also, than ten thousand words in an unknown tongue. 26 . . . Let all things be done unto edifying. Also v. 31.*

### d. Recognizing the fact that God does not give the same gifts to everyone.

Romans 12:3-8

*3 For I say, through the grace given unto me, to every man that is among you, not to think of himself more highly than he ought to think; but to think soberly, according as God has dealt to every man the measure of faith.*
*4 For as we have many members in one body, and all members have not the same office:*
*5 So we, being many, are one body in Christ, and every one members one of another.*
*6 Having then gifts differing according to the grace that is given to us, whether prophecy, let us prophesy according to the proportion of faith;*
*7 Or ministry, let us wait on our ministering: or he that teacheth, on teaching;*
*8 Or he that exhorteth, on exhortation: he that giveth, let him do it with simplicity; he that ruleth, with diligence; he that sheweth mercy, with cheerfulness.*

1 Corinthians 12:4-31

*4 Now there are diversities of gifts, but the same Spirit. [v. 8-10 list various gifts.] 11 But all these worketh that one and the selfsame Spirit, dividing to every man severally as he will. [Another list of gifted persons in v. 28-30].*

### e. Placing love above ability to speak

1 Corinthians 13:1, 2,

*1 Though I speak with the tongues of men and of angels, and have not charity [love], I am become as sounding brass or a tinkling cymbal. 2 And though I have the gift of prophecy, and understand all mysteries, and all knowledge; and though I have all faith, so that I could remove mountains, and have not charity [love], I am nothing.*

## 7. We must be responsible for what we say.

Psalm 19:14

David's prayer: *14 Let the words of my mouth and the meditation of my heart be acceptable in thy sight, O Lord, my strength, and my redeemer.*

Matthew 12:36

*But I say unto you, That every idle word that men shall speak, they shall give account thereof in the day of judgment.*

In addition, many Scriptures quoted elsewhere in this chapter.

# VI. Concerning God's speaking

## 1. When God speaks, things happen.

Genesis 1:3

*And God said, Let there be light: and there was light.*

Also 1:6-8, 9, 11, 14, 20, 24, 26, 29.

Numbers 27:12-14 and Deuteronomy 34:5

God promises that Moses is to die before entering the land: *34:5 So Moses the servant of the Lord died there in the land of Moab, according to the word of the Lord.*

Psalm 33:6, 9; also 148:5

*6 By the word of the Lord were the heavens made; and all the host of them by the breath of his mouth.*
*9 For he spake, and it was done; he commanded, and it stood fast.*

104:7, 8

At God's rebuke the waters which once covered the mountains  receded to the valleys.

Jeremiah 10:13

*When he uttereth his voice, there is a multitude of waters in the heavens, and he causeth the vapors to ascend from the ends of the earth; he maketh light-nings with rain, and bringeth forth the wind out of his treasures.* Also 51:16.

Daniel 4:30-33

*30 The king [Nebuchadnezzar] spake, and said, Is not this great Babylon, that I have built for the house of the kingdom . . . ? 31 While the word was in the king's mouth, there fell a voice from heaven, saying, O king Nebuchadnezzar, to thee it is spoken; The kingdom is departed from thee . . . . 33 The same hour was the thing fulfilled . . . .*

John 2:7-11

*7 Jesus saith unto them, Fill the waterpots with water . . . . 8 . . . Draw out now, and bear unto the governor of the feast. And they bare it. 9 When the ruler . . . had tasted the water that was made wine . . . 10 . . . [he said] thou hast kept the good wine until now. 11 This beginning of miracles did Jesus in Cana . . . .*

5:8, 9

*8 Jesus saith unto him, Rise, take up thy bed, and walk. 9 And immediately the man was made whole . . . .*

Also 9:7, the blind man healed at Jesus' word; and 11:43, 44, the raising of Lazarus at His word; and many other miracles where Christ spoke and something happened.

1 Thessalonians 4:16, 17

Yet future: *16 For the Lord himself shall descend from heaven with a shout, with the voice of the archangel, and with the trump of God: and the dead in Christ shall rise first; 17 Then we which are alive and remain shall be caught up together with them in the clouds, to meet the Lord in the air; and so shall we ever be with the Lord.*

Hebrews 11:3

*Through faith we understand that the worlds [literally, ages] were framed by the word of God . . . .*

PROJECT: Study some of the specific prophecies, where God spoke in judgment concerning some nation or city; then find the fulfillment in ancient history. For example, read the prophecies concerning the city of Tyre in Ezekiel 26, 27, along with the description of the city as it was at the time. Note the sins for which God pronounced judgment, and the details of the judgment. Consult history and archeology books to find out what happened. Find a presentday description of the same area now.

---

**Books are standing counselors and preachers, always at hand, and always disinterested; having this advantage over oral instructors, that they are ready to repeat their lesson as often as we please.**

-- **Talbot Chambers**
1819-1896

## 2. When God speaks, He keeps His word.

A few examples:

Genesis 9:11-17

God speaking to Noah: *11 And I will establish my covenant with you; neither shall all flesh be cut off any more by the waters of a flood; neither shall there be any more flood to destroy the earth. 12 And God said, This is the token of the covenant which I make between me and you and every living creature that is with you, for perpetual generations: 13 I do set my bow in the cloud . . . 15 And I will remember my covenant . . . .*

Genesis 12:1, 2; 15:4; 17:15, 16; 21:1

*1 Now the Lord had said unto Abram, Get thee out of thy country . . . unto a land that I will shew thee: 2 And I will make of thee a great nation . . . .*

After Ishmael's birth: *4 And behold the word of the Lord came unto him saying, This shall not be thine heir; but he that shall come forth out of thine own bowels [or, body, NASB] shall be thine heir.*

*And God said to Abraham, As for Sarai thy wife . . . 16 . . . I will bless her, and give thee a son of her . . . and she shall be a mother of nations . . . 19 And God said, Sarah thy wife shall bear thee a son indeed; and thou shalt call his name Isaac: and I will establish my covenant with him . . . .*

*And the Lord visited Sarah as he had said, and the Lord did unto Sarah as he had spoken.*

Exodus 3:8

God speaking to Moses: *8 And I am come to deliver them [Israel] out of the hand of the Egyptians . . . .* Exodus 12:29-36 tells of the fulfilment.

Joshua 6:2, 20, 21

*2 And the Lord said unto Joshua, See, I have given unto thine hand Jericho . . . . 20 . . . they took the city 21 And they utterly destroyed all that was in the city.*

Jeremiah 31:36, 37

*36 If those ordinances* [God speaking of the ordinances of the moon and stars] *depart from before me, saith the Lord, then the seed of Israel also shall cease from being a nation before me for ever. 37 Thus saith the Lord; If heaven above can be measured, and the foundations of the earth searched out beneath, I will also cast off all the seed of Israel for all that they have done, saith the Lord.*

33:20, 21

*Thus saith the Lord; If ye can break my covenant of the day, and my covenant of the night, and that there should not be day and night in their season; 21 Then may also my covenant be broken with David my servant.* Also v. 25, 26.

Ezekiel 12:25

God speaking of the coming judgment of Jerusalem: *25 For I am the Lord: I will speak, and the word that I speak shall come to pass; it shall be no more prolonged: for in your days, O rebellious house, will I say the word, and will perform it, saith the Lord God.* Also v. 26-28; Also v. 26-28; 22:14-16; 24:14.

21:28-32

God promises judgment to the Ammonites: *31 And I will pour out mine indignation upon thee, I will blow against thee in the fire of my wrath, and deliver thee into the hand of brutish men, and skillful to destroy. 32 Thou shalt be for fuel to the fire; thy blood shall be in the midst of the land; thou shalt be no more remembered; for I the Lord have spoken it.*

## 3. When God speaks, we must pay attention.

Deuteronomy 8:3

*. . . Man doth not live by bread only, but by every word that proceedeth out of the mouth of the Lord doth man live.* Also Matthew 4:4.

Nehemiah 8:1-18

The example of the people of Israel in Ezra's day. They listened to the Word and then did something about what they heard.

Psalm 85:8

The determination of the Psalmist: *8 I will hear what God the Lord will speak . . . .*

Proverbs 28:9

*He that turneth away his ear from hearing the law,* *even his prayer shall be abomination.*

Jeremiah 29:17-19

God describes the coming judgment upon Jerusalem (17, 18) *19 Because they have not hearkened to my words, saith the Lord, which I sent unto them by my servants the prophets, rising up early and sending them; but ye would not hear, saith the Lord.*

Hosea 9:17

God's judgment of Israel shows the seriousness with which He considers failure to listen to Him. *17 My God will cast them away, because they did not hearken unto him: and they shall be wanderers among the nations.*

Romans 10:17

> *So then faith cometh by hearing, and hearing by the word of God.*

Hebrews 2:1-4

> *1 Therefore we ought to give the more earnest heed to the things which we have heard, lest at any time we should let them slip.*

12:25, 26

> *25 See that ye refuse not him that speaketh. For if they escaped not who refused him that spake on earth, much more shall not we escape, if we turn away from him that speaketh from heaven: 26 Whose voice then shook the earth: but now he hath promised, saying, Yet once more I shake not the earth only, but also heaven.*

## 4. When God speaks, we cannot answer, but only submit.

Job 9:14-16

> Job speaking: *14 How much less shall I answer him, and choose out my words to reason with him? 15 Whom, though I were righteous, yet would I not answer, but I would make supplication to my judge. 16 If I had called, and he had answered me; yet would I not believe that he had hearkened unto my name.* Job makes this statement in spite of the fact that in Chapter 10 he is discouraged and puzzled at God's dealings.

38:1-4

> *1 Then the Lord answered Job out of the whirlwind, and said, 2 Who is this that darkeneth counsel without knowledge? 3 Gird up now thy loins like a man; for I will demand of thee, and answer thou me.* In the rest of Chapter 38 and 39 is a list of questions God asked Job, for which he had no answer .

40:1-5

> *1 Moreover the Lord answered Job, and said, 2 Shall he that contendeth with the Almighty instruct him? he that reproveth God, let him answer it. 3 Then Job answered the Lord and said, 4 Behold, I am vile; what shall I answer thee? I will lay mine hand upon my*

*mouth. 5 Once have I spoken; but I will not answer: yea, twice, but I will proceed no further.* Chapters 40 and 41 continue with God's unanswerable questions.

Isaiah 6:8

> Isaiah's testimony; *8 Also I heard the voice of the Lord saying, Whom shall I send, and who will go for us? Then said I, Here am I; send me.*

Matthew 4:18-20

> *18 And Jesus, walking by the sea of Galilee, saw two brethren, Simon called Peter, and Andrew his brother, casting a net into the sea: for they were fishers. 19 And he saith unto them, Follow me, and I will make you fishers of men. 20 And they straightway left their nets and followed him.*

> Also true of James and John: verses 21, 22; and Matthew, in 9:9.

PROJECT: As you study Jeremiah, note some of the things that God asked him to do to portray His message. In each case Jeremiah's only answer was submission and obedience. For example, look at Jeremiah 13:1-11; 16:1-4; 27:1-11; 32:6-15.

---

### QUOTES TO QUOTE

CAN APES REALLY TALK? After 5 years and $250,000, Columbia University professor, Dr. Herbert Terrace has concluded they cannot. Although they learn dozens of signs, they can't compose sentences, and apparently only mimic their teachers.

Reported in Associates for Biblical Research Newsletter
April, 1980

Thinking cannot be clear till it has had expression. We must write, or speak, or act our thoughts, or they will remain in a half torpid form. Our feelings must have expression, or they will be as clouds, which, till they descend as rain, will never bring up fruit or flower. So it is with the inward feelings; expression gives them development.

Henry Ward Beecher
1813-1887

Those who have but little business to attend to are great talkers. The less men think, the more they talk.

Charles Montesquieu
1689-1755

# 6

# Listening

## CONCEPT SUMMARY

1. The ability to hear is a gift from God.
2. Listening is basic to much of learning and awareness.
3. Hearing is often the first step to a major change in our lives.
4. Listening is a source of pleasure and fellowship.
5. Listening demands response.
6. When God speaks, we must listen and obey.
7. Those who belong to God recognize His voice.
8. Refusal to listen to God's messenger is also refusal to listen to God.
9. When we refuse to listen to the truth from God, we are quick to believe that which is not true - to turn to fables and lies.
10. Our ability to hear and understand depends on our previous attention to truth.
11. We are responsible to listen to and obey parents.
12. We are responsible to listen to and submit to those whom God has placed over us in various capacities.
13. We are wise to listen carefully to the reproof and counsel of others.
14. We must consider carefully who speaks and what is said.
15. We must evaluate what we hear by the Word of God.
16. We must not believe all we hear.
17. Our listening should contribute to wholesome Christian thinking and living; we are responsible for what we listen to.

18. The almighty, eternal God of the universe listens to man, his creation - incredible but true!

19. As God listens to us, we should listen to others.

## TRY THESE

**SEE HOW CHRIST LISTENED. Again and again in His ministry, the Lord listened to people and responded to their needs. Go through the Gospel of Luke, or some part of it, noting all the needs to which He responded. His ministry was only three and a half years long, yet He had time to listen.**

**PRACTICE LISTENING. From time to time read a short story, or the account of an incident to your class, asking them to listen as carefully as possible. Follow with a quick quiz. You may wish to do this repeatedly over a period of time, keeping scores and challenging pupils to improve.**

**PREPARE A BULLETIN BOARD. As a follow-up of some project or study related to listening, select a committee to prepare a bulletin board entitled, "We are glad we can hear . . . ."**

## THINK ABOUT THESE

Lenin . . . allegedly instructed his followers to first confuse the vocabulary . . . He knew that thinking can be done only in words and that accurate thinking requires words of precise meaning. Confuse the vocabulary, and the unsuspecting majority is at a disadvantage when defending themselves against the small but highly disciplined minority which knows exactly what it wants and which deliberately promotes word-confusion as the first step in its efforts to divide and conquer.

> -- Henry Grady Weaver, *The Mainspring of Human Progress*
> (Irvington-on-Hudson, NY: Foundation for Economic Education, Ing.,
> 1953. p. 256. As quoted in *Christian Teacher*, July, August, September,
> 1966. p. 77.

A single conversation across the table with a wise man is worth a month's study of books.    -- A Chinese proverb

If you light upon an impertinent talker, that sticks to you like a burr, deal freely with him, break off the discourse, and pursue your business.

> -- Plutarch
> 46-120 A.D.

The reason why so few people are agreeable in conversation is that each is thinking more of what he is intending to say, than of what others are saying; and we never listen when we are planning to speak.

> -- Francois Rochefoucauld
> 1630-1680

## SCRIPTURAL BACKGROUND

### 1. The ability to hear is a gift from God.

Exodus 4:11

*And the Lord said unto him [Moses], Who hath made man's mouth? or who maketh the dumb, or deaf . . . ? have not I the Lord?*

Psalm 94:9

It is God *"that planteth the ear"* in man.

Proverbs 20:12

*The hearing ear and the seeing eye, the Lord hath made even both of them.*

1 Corinthians 12:16-18

*16 And if the ear shall say, Because I am not the eye, I am not of the body; is it therefore not of the body? 17 If the whole body were an eye, where were the hearing? If the whole were hearing, where were the smelling? 18 But now hath God set the members every one of them in the body, as it hath pleased him.*

### 2. Listening is basic to much of learning and awareness.

Psalm 34:11

David speaking after testifying to God's goodness: *11 Come, ye children, hearken unto me: I will teach you the fear of the Lord.*

44:1

*We have heard with our ears, O God, our fathers have told us, what work thou didst in their days, in the times of old.* Also Psalm 78:1-4

Proverbs 8:32-34

Wisdom speaking: *32 Now therefore hearken unto me, O ye children: for blessed are they that keep my ways. 33 Hear instruction, and be wise, and refuse it not. 34*

*Blessed is the man that heareth me . . . . In Christ are hid all the treasures of wisdom and knowledge.* Colossians 2:3.

15:31-33

*31 The ear that heareth the reproof of life abideth among the wise. 32 He that refuseth instruction despiseth his own soul: but he that heareth reproof getteth understanding. 33 The fear of the Lord is the instruction of wisdom . . . .*

18:15

*. . . The ear of the wise seeketh knowledge.*

Isaiah 50:4 (NASB)

*The Lord God . . . awakens Me morning by morning. He awakens My ear to listen as a disciple* [or, learner]. This statement undoubtedly refers particularly to Christ. Even He listened to the Father on a regular basis.

1 Timothy 1:13

*Hold fast the form of sound words which thou hast heard of me, in faith and love which is in Christ Jesus.*

## 3. Hearing is often the first step to a major change in our lives.

Genesis 6:13, 14

*13 And God said unto Noah, The end of all flesh is come before me; . . . I will destroy them with the earth. 14 Make thee an ark of gopher wood . . . .* When Noah heard this command, his major life project was set.

12:1-4

When God spoke to Abram, His command meant a long journey, a leaving of family whom he would probably never see again, living in a strange land in tents. Look up Ur of the Chaldees to learn how much of a change in culture an environment was involved. *1 Now the Lord had said unto Abram, Get thee out of thy country, and from thy kindred, and from thy father's house, unto a land that I will shew thee: . . . 4 So Abram departed, as the Lord had spoken unto him . . . .*

2 Kings 22:11-20; 23:1-27

When King Josiah heard the Word read, he repented himself first, and then called together the leaders of Judah and the people for a public reading of the Law. The people too repented. This hearing of the Word resulted in the destruction of much of the idol worship and a restoration of the proper worship of the Lord - a changed nation, at least for a time.

Nehemiah 8:1-18; 9:1-3

When Israel heard the Book of the Law read to them they were changed. Note especially their rejoicing (8:12), their obedience in making and dwelling in booths (8:14-18), their confession of sin and worship of the Lord (9:1-3).

Luke 8:4-15

The parable of the sower. *15 But that on the good ground are they which in an honest and good heart, having heard the word, keep it, and bring forth fruit.* Fruitfulness begins with hearing and obeying.

Acts 2:4-6, 41

On the Day of Pentecost: *4 And they were all filled with the Holy Ghost and began to speak with other tongues . . . . 6 Now when this was noised abroad, the multitude came together, and were confounded, because that every man heard them speak in his own language . . . . 41 Then they that gladly received his [Peter's] word were baptized: and the same day there were added unto them about three thousand souls.* The multitude was changed as they heard the Gospel.

8:5-8, 26-40

Philip was involved in successful evangelistic preaching in Samaria when he heard God speak (v. 26); he obeyed and found the Ethiopian ready to receive Christ. Philip's activity was changed as God spoke to him; the Ethiopian too was changed as he heard the message.

Romans 10:17

*So then faith cometh by hearing, and hearing by the word of God.*

Ephesians 4:29

Hearing brings grace to the hearers - thus changed lives.

James 1:18, 19

*18 Of his* [the Father's] *own will begat he us with the word of truth . . . . 19 Wherefore, my beloved brethren, let every man be swift to hear . . . .*

## 4. Listening is a source of pleasure and fellowship.

1 Samuel 16:23

*And it came to pass, when the evil spirit from God was upon Saul, that David took an harp, and played with his hand: so Saul was refreshed, and was well, and the evil spirit departed from him.*

1 Samuel 18-20

The account of the fellowship between David and Jonathan indicates that they listened to one another and appreciated one another. *20:42 And Jonathan said to David, Go in peace, forasmuch as we have sworn both of us in the name of the Lord, saying, The Lord be between me and thee, and between my seed and thy seed forever.*

Psalm 143:8

David's desire to hear from God: *8 Cause me to hear thy lovingkindness in the morning, for in thee do I trust: cause me to know the way wherein I should walk, for I lift up my soul unto thee.*

Isaiah 55:3

God's eagerness for us to listen to Him: *3 Incline your ear, and come unto me: hear, and your soul shall live; and I will make an everlasting covenant with you, even the sure mercies of David.* [Spoken to Israel in particular.]

Jeremiah 15:16

Jeremiah's testimony: *16 Thy words were found, and I did eat them; and thy word was unto me the joy and rejoicing of mine heart.*

## 5. Listening demands response.

Exodus 24:7

An example: *7 And he [Moses] took the book of the covenant, and read in the audience of the people: and they said, All that the Lord hath said will we do, and be obedient.*

35:4, 5, 29 and 36:4, 5

An example: *4 And Moses spake unto all the congregation of the children of Israel, saying, This is the thing which the Lord commanded, saying, 5 Take ye from among you an offering unto the Lord: whosoever is of a willing heart, let him bring it . . . . 29 The children of Israel brought a willing offering unto the Lord, every man and woman, whose heart made them willing . . . . 36:4 And all the wise men, that wrought all the work of the sanctuary, came every man from his work which they made; 5 And they spake unto Moses, saying, The people bring much more than enough . . . .*

2 Kings 22:11-20; 23:1-27

The response of Josiah and then the people of Israel to the reading of the Law. Also 2 Chronicles 34:29-33; 35:1-19.

Nehemiah 9:13, 16, 17, 30

As a response to the reading of the Law in Ezra's day,

Colossians 1:3-9

The basis of Paul's prayers for the Colossian church was what he had heard of their faith. *3 We give thanks to God . . . praying always for you. 4 Since we heard of your faith in Christ Jesus . . . . 8 [Epaphras] also declared unto us your love in the Spirit. 9 For this cause we also, since the day we heard it, do not cease to pray for you . . . .*

3 John 3, 4

Similarly John rejoiced because of what he had heard.

the priests and Levites confessed Israel's repeated failure to obey God:

*13 Thou [God] camest down also upon mount Sinai, and spakest with them from heaven . . . 16 But they [Israel] and our fathers dealt proudly, and hardened their necks, and hearkened not to thy commandments, 17 And refused to obey . . . . 30 Yet many years didst thou forbear them, and testifiedst against them by thy spirit in thy prophets: yet would they not give ear: therefore gavest thou them into the hand of the people of the land.*

Luke 11:28

*. . . Yea rather, blessed are they that hear the word of God and keep it.*

James 1:22-25

*22 But be ye doers of the word, and not hearers only, deceiving your own selves. 23 For if any be a hearer of the word, and not a doer, he is like unto a man beholding his natural face in a glass: 24 For he beholdeth himself, and goeth his way, and straightway forgetteth what manner of man he was. 25 But whoso looketh into the perfect law of liberty, and continueth therein, he being not a forgetful hearer, but a doer of the work, this man shall be blessed in his deed.*

## 6. When God speaks, we must listen and obey.

1 Samuel 3:1-21

An example: The account of the boy Samuel's listening to God, even in a difficult circumstance.

15:22, 23

A negative example. Samuel speaking to King Saul after Saul had disobeyed God: *22 And Samuel said, Hath the Lord as great delight in burnt offerings and sacrifices, as in obeying the voice of the Lord? Behold, to obey is better than sacrifice, and to hearken than the fat of rams. 23 . . . Because thou hast rejected the word of the Lord, he hath also rejected thee from being*

king.

Proverbs 28:9

*He that turneth away his ear from hearing the law, even his prayer shall be abomination.*

Ecclesiastes 5:1

Solomon speaking in old age: *1 Keep thy foot when thou goest to the house of God, and be more ready to hear, than to give the sacrifice of fools . . . .*

Jeremiah 29:17-19

God considers failure to listen and obey Him a serious

sin: *17 Thus saith the Lord of hosts; Behold, I will send upon them the sword, the famine, and the pestilence . . . 18 And I will persecute them . . . 19 Because they have not hearkened to my words, saith the Lord . . . .*

### Ezekiel 3:10, 11

God's expectation of the prophet Ezekiel: *10 . . . Son of man, all my words that I shall speak unto thee, receive in thine heart and hear with thine ears, 11 And go get thee to them of the captivity . . . and speak unto the.*

### 33:30-33

God describes Israel as a people that pretend to hear His message but refuse to obey. His description fits many people who outwardly listen: *32 And lo, thou [i.e., Ezekiel the prophet] art unto them as a very lovely song of one that hath a pleasant voice, and can play well on an instrument: for they hear thy words, but they do them not.*

### 44:5

God instructs Ezekiel to listen well and watch all that God says and shows, and to mark well all His ordinances.

### The Book of Jonah

Both a negative and a positive example. The record of Jonah's refusal to obey God, his experiences under God's chastening, and his later carrying out of God's command illustrate well the importance of obedience.

### Matthew 7:24-27

*24 Therefore whoever heareth these sayings of mine, and doeth them, I will liken unto a wise man, which built his house upon a rock.*

### Matthew 11:15

Jesus speaking: *15 He that hath ears to hear, let him hear.*

### Mark 7:14, 16

The Lord speaking: *14 . . . Hearken unto me, every one of you, and understand . . . 16 If any man have ears to hear, let him hear.*

### Revelation 2:7

Christ speaking to the church at Ephesus: *7 He that hath an ear, let him hear what the Spirit saith unto the churches . . . .* Also 2:11, 17, 29; 3:6, 13, 22.

## 7. Those who belong to God recognize His voice.

### Genesis 3:8

*And they heard the voice of the Lord God walking in the garden in the cool of the day: and Adam and his wife hid themselves from the presence of the Lord God amongst the trees of the garden.*

### Judges 6:12, 13

Gideon recognized God speaking to him: *12 And the angel of the Lord appeared unto him, and said unto him, The Lord is with thee, thou mighty man of valour. 13 And Gideon said unto him, Oh my Lord, if the Lord be with us, why then is all this befallen us? . . .*

### John 8:43, 44, 47

Jesus speaking to the Jews: *43 Why do ye not understand my speech? even because ye cannot hear my word. 44 Ye are of your father the devil . . . . 47 He that is of God heareth God's words: ye therefore hear them not, because ye are not of God.*

### 10:4, 5, 16, 26-28

Jesus speaking: *4 And when he putteth forth his own sheep, he goeth before them, and the sheep follow him: for they know his voice. 5 And a stranger will they not follow, but will flee from him: for they know not the voice of a stranger . . . .*

*16 And other sheep I have, which are not of this fold: them also I must bring, and they shall hear my voice; and there shall be one fold, and one shepherd.*

*26 But ye believe not, because ye are not my sheep, as I said unto you. 27 My sheep hear my voice, and I know them, and they follow me: 28 And I give unto them eternal life . . . .*

### Acts 27:23-25

Paul recognized the fact that it was God speaking to him in the storm-tossed ship: *23 For there stood by me this night the angel of God, whose I am, and whom I serve, 24 Saying, Fear not, Paul; thou must be brought before Caesar: and, lo, God hath given thee all them that sail with thee. 25 Wherefore, sirs, be of good cheer: for I believe God, that it shall be even as it was told me.*

### 1 John 4:5, 6

John contrasts false teachers, not of God, and those who are of God, and hear the Word.

### Revelation 3:20

An invitation: *20 Behold, I stand at the door and knock: if any man hear my voice, and open the door, I will come in to him, and will sup with him, and he with me.*

**No matter how crowded our schedule, we had better put at the top of it, "It is time to seek the Lord." There will not be blessing until we take time for His direction in all our work.**

**-- Harold Duff**

### 8. Refusal to listen to God's messenger is also refusal to listen to God.

Jeremiah 44:4-6

*4 Howbeit I sent unto you all my servants the prophets, rising early and sending them . . . 5 But they hearkened not, nor inclined their ear to turn from their wickedness . . . 6 Wherefore my fury and mine anger was poured forth . . . .*  Also 15, 16, 20-23

Ezekiel 3:7

God speaking to the prophet Ezekiel:*7 But the house of Israel will not hearken unto thee; for they will not hearken unto me: for all the house of Israel are impudent and hardhearted.*

33:7-9

The Lord speaking to Ezekiel: *7 So thou, O son of man, I have set thee a watchman unto the house of Israel; therefore thou shalt hear the word at my mouth, and warn them from me. 8 When I say unto the wicked, O wicked man, thou shalt surely die; if thou dost not speak to warn the wicked from his way, that wicked man shall die in his iniquity: but his blood will I require at thy hand. 9 Nevertheless, if thou warn the wicked on his way to turn from it; if he do not turn from his way, he shall die in his iniquity; but thou hast delivered thy soul.*

Luke 10:16

Jesus speaking to the seventy: *16 He that heareth you heareth me; and he that despiseth you despiseth me; and he that despiseth me despiseth him that sent me.*

### 9. When we refuse to listen to the truth from God, we are quick to believe that which is not true - to turn to fables and lies.

2 Thessalonians 2:10-12

*10 . . . They received not the truth that they might be saved. 11 And for this cause God shall send them strong delusion, that they should believe a lie: 12 That they all might be damned who believed not the truth, but had pleasure in unrighteousness.*

2 Timothy 4:3, 4

*3 For the time will come when they will not endure sound doctrine [or, teaching]; but after their own lusts shall they heap to themselves teachers, having itching ears; 4 And they shall turn away their ears from the truth, and shall be turned to fables.*

(NASB) *3 For the time will come when they will not endure sound doctrine; but wanting to have their ears tickled, they will accumulate for themselves teachers in accordance to their own desires; 4 and will turn away their ears from the truth, and will turn aside to myths.*

See also Romans 1:18-32

### 10. Our ability to hear and understand depends on our previous attention to truth.

Genesis 22:1-3

Abraham's response to God in this test was based on many previous experiences with listening and responding to God.

Matthew 13:15, 16 (NASB)

Christ quoting Isaiah in explanation of his speaking in parables: *15 For the heart of this people has become dull, and with their ears they can scarcely hear, And they have closed their eyes Lest they should see with their eyes, and hear with their ears, And understand with their heart and turn again, And I should heal them. 16 But blessed are your eyes, because they see; and your ears, because they hear.*

John 8:30-32

*30 As He [Jesus] spake these words, many believed on him. 31 Then said Jesus to those Jews which believed on him, If ye continue in my word, then are you my disciples indeed; 32 And ye shall know the truth and the truth shall make you free.*  Also 7:17.

Hebrews 5:11-14

*11 Of whom [i.e., Melchisedec] we have many things to say, and hard to be uttered, seeing ye are dull of hearing. 12 For when for the time ye ought to be teachers, ye have need that one teach you again which be the first principles of the oracles of God; and are become such as have need of milk, and not of strong meat. 13 For every one that useth milk is unskilful in the word of righteousness: for he is a babe. 14 But strong meat belongeth to them that are of full age, even those who by reason of use have their senses exercised to discern both good and evil.*

See also 1 Corinthians 3:1-4

**Habit is a cable; we weave a thread of it every day, until at last it becomes so strong we cannot break it.**

-- Horace Greeley, 1811-1872

## 11. We are responsible to listen to and obey parents.

### a. God gives parents responsibility for the behavior of their children.

Genesis 18:19

God speaking of Abraham: *19 For I know him, that he will command his children and his household after him, and they shall keep the way of the Lord, to do justice and judgment; that the Lord may bring upon Abraham that which he hath spoken of him.*

Deuteronomy 21:18-21

Here, under the Law, if a son was stubborn and rebellious, and refused to listen to his parents, they were responsible to take him bodily to the elders of the city for stoning. While this is not the New Testament pattern, it shows the great responsibility given to parents, and the seriousness with which God regards rebelliousness.

1 Samuel 3:13

When God pronounced judgment upon Eli, it was for not restraining his sons, even though they were no longer little boys. *13 For I have told him that I will judge his house for ever for the iniquity which he knoweth; because his sons made themselves vile, and he restrained them not.* See 2:12-17.

Proverbs 13:24

*He that spareth his rod hateth his son: but he that loveth him chasteneth him betimes.* Also 23:13, 14.

19:18

*Chasten thy son while there is hope, and let not thy soul spare for his crying.*

22:6

*Train up a child in the way he should go: and when he is old, he will not depart from it.*

29:15, 17

*15 The rod and reproof give wisdom: but a child left to himself bringeth his mother to shame. 17 Correct thy son, and he shall give thee rest; yea, he shall give delight unto thy soul.*

Ephesians 6:4

*And ye fathers, provoke not your children to wrath: but bring them up in the nurture and admonition of the Lord.* Also Colossians 3:21.

1 Timothy 3:4, 5, 12

One qualification of a pastor or deacon is that his children behave well, and in submission to their father.

### b. God commands children to hearken to their parents, and commends those who do so.

Proverbs 1:8, 9

*8 My son, hear the instruction of thy father, and forsake not the law of thy mother. 9 For they [i.e., the instruction] shall be an ornament of grace unto thy head, and chains about thy neck.* Also 4:1-4; 6:20-22.

3:1, 2

God promises reward: *1 My son, forget not my law; but let thine heart keep my commandments: 2 For length of days, and long life, and peace.* Also Exodus 20:12.

6:20-22

*20 My son, keep thy father's commandment, and forsake not the law of thy mother ... 22 When thou goest, it shall lead thee; when thou sleepest, it shall keep thee;*

*and when thou awakest, it shall talk with thee.* [Note the all-pervading influence described]

15:5

*A fool despiseth his fathers instruction . . . .*

23:22

*Hearken unto thy father that begat thee, and despise not thy mother when she is old.*

Ephesians 6:1

*Children, obey your parents in the Lord: for this is right.*

Colossians 3:20

*Children, obey your parent in all things: for this is well pleasing unto the Lord.*

## 12. We are responsible to listen to and submit to those whom God has placed over us in various capacities.

Joshua 22:2, 5

Joshua commends those who settled on the east of Jordan for their obedience to Moses, and encourages their continued obedience to his commands:

*2 . . . Ye have kept all that Moses the servant of the Lord commanded you, and have obeyed my voice in all that I commanded you. 5 Take diligent heed to do the commandment and the law, which Moses the servant of the Lord charged you, to love the Lord your God, and to walk in all his ways . . . .*

Proverbs 5:1-13

Verses 12, 13 express a common lament of a young person who has refused to listen and thus has become involved in sin: *12 How have I hated instruction, and my heart despised reproof; 13 And have not obeyed the voice of my teachers, nor inclined mine ear to them that instructed me.*

Note that this expression of regret follows a warning to young men to pay attention to instruction(v. 1, 7), and especially to beware of immorality and its resulting disgrace (v. 9), financial loss (v. 10), and venereal disease (v. 11).

Philippians 4:9

Paul commands obedience: *9 Those things, which ye have both learned, and received, and heard, and seen in me, do: and the God of peace shall be with you.*

Hebrews 13:7

*Remember them that have the rule over you [i.e., your guides], who have spoken unto you the word of God: whose faith follow, considering the end of their conversation [way of life].*

13:17

*Obey them that have the rule over you and submit yourselves: for they watch for your souls, as they that must give account, that they may do it with joy, and not with grief: for that is unprofitable for you.*

(NASB) *Obey your leaders, and submit to them; for they keep watch over your souls . . . .*

See also Romans 13:1-7; Colossians 3:18, 20, 22; 1 Timothy 6:1, 2; 1 Peter 3:1-6; 5:5. These verses do not mention listening specifically, but do teach submission to those in authority over us. In doing so, they imply listening!

## 13 . We are wise to listen carefully to the reproof and counsel of others.

Genesis 41:1-57

Pharaoh gave heed to the counsel of Joseph as he gave God's interpretation of Pharaoh's dream. By doing so, he saved Egypt, and Israel too.

*29 Behold there come seven years of great plenty throughout all the land of Egypt: 30 And there shall arise after them seven years of famine . . . . 37 And the thing was good in the eyes of Pharaoh, and in the eyes of all his servants . . . . 57 And all countries came into Egypt to Joseph to buy corn . . . .*

Proverbs 11:14

*Where no counsel is the people fall: but in the multitude of counsellors there is safety.*

12:15

*The way of a fool is right in his own eyes: but he that hearkeneth unto counsel is wise.*

15:5

*. . . He that regardeth reproof is prudent.* Also 15: 31, 32.

29:1

*He, that being often reproved hardeneth his neck, shall suddenly be destroyed, and that without remedy.*

Hebrews 12:11

*Now no chastening for the present seemeth to be joyous, but grievous: nevertheless afterward it yieldeth the peaceable fruit of righteousness unto them which are exercised thereby.*

Revelation 3:19

Christ speaking to the church: *19 As many as I love, I rebuke and chasten: be zealous therefore, and repent.*

## 14. We must consider carefully who speaks and what is said.

Genesis 39:7-12

The example of Joseph in refusing to listen to Potiphar's wife.

1 Kings 11:1-19

Rehoboam, son of Solomon, refused to listen to the counsel of the older men (v. 8), who represented the people, and as a result caused the kingdom to be divided (v. 18, 19).

2 Chronicles 18

Jehosophat listened to Ahab and prophets. As a result, except for the Lord's intervention, he would have lost his life (v. 31).

Psalm 1:1

*Blessed is the man that walketh not in the counsel of the ungodly . . . .*

Proverbs 7:1-27

A warning against listening to the enticing words of a prostitute. Note her speech: flattery (v. 5, 21), pretense of piety (v. 14), interest in him (v. 15), description of her bedroom (v. 16, 17), direct invitation to sin (v. 18), assurance of her husband's continued absence (v. 19, 20).

*25 Let not thine heart decline to her ways, go not astray in her paths.*

17:4

*A wicked doer giveth heed to false lips, and a liar giveth ear to a naughty tongue.*

20:19

*He that goeth about as a talebearer revealeth secrets: therefore meddle not with him that flattereth with his lips.*

(NASB) *He who goes about as a slanderer reveals secrets, Therefore do not associate with a gossip.*

26:24, 25 (NASB)

*24 He who hates disguises it with his lips, But he lays up deceit in his heart. 25 When he speaks graciously, do not believe him, For there are seven abominations in his heart.*

29:12

*If a ruler hearken to lies, all his servants are wicked.*

Isaiah 30:1, 2

*1 Woe to the rebellious children, saith the Lord, that take counsel, but not of me . . . 2 That walk to go down into Egypt, and have not asked at my mouth . . . .*

Jeremiah 23:16

*Thus saith the Lord of hosts, Hearken not unto the words of the prophets . . . they make you vain: they speak a vision of their own heart and not out of the mouth of the Lord.* Also 29:15-19.

Luke 21:8

*And he [Christ] said, Take heed that ye be not deceived: for many shall come in my name, saying, I am Christ; and the time draweth near: go ye not therefore after them.*

Ephesians 5:6, 7

*6 Let no man deceive you with vain words: for because of these things cometh the wrath of God upon the children of disobedience. 7 Be not ye therefore partakers with them.*

2 Timothy 2:16

*But shun profane and vain babblings: for they will increase unto more ungodliness.*

## 15. We must evaluate what we hear by the Word of God.

Proverbs 19:27

*Cease, my son, to hear the instuction that causeth thee to err from the words of knowledge.*

Jeremiah 27:9, 10

After God had said, in verse 8, that they would serve Babylon, Jeremiah continued with God's message: *9 Therefore hearken not ye to your prophets, nor to your enchanters, which speak unto you, saying, Ye shall not serve the king of Babylon. 10 For they prophecy a lie to you . . . .* Also 29:8-10.

Isaiah 8:20

*To the law and to the testimony: if they speak not according to this word, it is because there is no light in them.*

Acts 17:11, 12

A worthy example: *11 These [i.e., the Christians at Berea] were more noble than those in Thessalonica, in that they received the word with all readiness of mind, and searched the scriptures daily, whether those things were so. 12 Therefore many of them believed . . . .*

Galatians 1:6-12

Paul expresses great concern that Christians not listen to those who pervert the Gospel. *9 . . . If any man preach any other gospel unto you than that ye have received, let him be accursed . . . 11 But I certify you, brethren, that the gospel which was preached of me is not after man. 12 For I neither received it of man, neither was I taught it, but by the revelation of Jesus Christ.*

Colossians 2:8

*Beware lest any man spoil you through philosophy and vain deceit, after the tradition of men, after the rudiments of the world, and not after Christ.*

1 John 4:1, 2

*1 Beloved, believe not every spirit, but try the spirits whether they are of God; because many false prophets are gone out into the world. 2 Hereby know ye the Spirit of God: Every spirit that confesseth that Jesus Christ is come in the flesh is of God.*

## 16. We must not believe all we hear.

Joshua 9:3-27

A negative example from which we can learn. The Gibeonites deceived Joshua and the men of Israel with their "hard luck story." *14 And the men took of their victuals, and asked not counsel at the mouth of the Lord. 15 And Joshua made peace with them, and made a league with them.*

Psalm 38:12-15

David's testimony at a time when he felt that nobody loved him: *12 They also that seek after my life lay snares for me: and they that seek my hurt speak mischievous things, and imagine deceits all the day long. 13 But I, as a deaf man, heard not; and I was as a dumb man that heareth not, and in whose mouth are no reproofs. 15 For in thee, O Lord, do I hope: thou wilt hear, O Lord my God.*

Ezekiel 14:10

Note in this passage that both the false prophet and the one who listens to him are to be punished alike: *10 And they* [prophets of idolatry] *shall bear the punishment of their iniquity: the punishment of the prophet shall be even as the punishment of him that seeketh unto him.*

Daneil 6:1-24

King Darius listened to his "cabinet" and as a result almost lost Daniel, his top man.

1 Timothy 1:4

*Neither give heed to fables and endless genealogies, which minister questions, rather than godly edifying, which is in faith.*

4:7

*But refuse profane and old wives' fables, and exercise thyself rather unto godliness.*

See also other Scripture included in Concepts 14 and 15.

## 17. Our listening should contribute to wholesome Christian thinking and living; we are responsible for what we listen to.

Proverbs 6:20-24

Listening to and heeding the Biblical teaching of godly parents, and keeping that teaching in our hearts will give guidance as we go through life day by day. It will protect from immorality.

*20 My son, keep thy father's commandment, and forsake not the law of thy mother: 21 Bind them continually upon thine heart, and tie them about thy neck. 22 When thou goest, it shall lead thee; when thou sleepest, it shall keep thee; and when thou awakest, it shall talk with thee. 23 For the commandment is a lamp; and the law is light; and reproofs of instruction are the way of life: 24 To keep thee from the evil woman, from the flattery of the tongue of a strange woman.*

Romans 6:11-13

*Likewise reckon* [or, consider] *ye also yourselves to be dead indeed unto sin, but alive unto God through Jesus Christ our Lord. 12 Let not sin therefore reign in your mortal body, that ye should obey it in the lusts thereof. 13 Neither yield ye your members as instruments of unrighteousness unto sin: but yield yourselves unto God, as those that are alive from the dead, and your members as instruments of righteousness unto God.* See also NASB.

12:1, 2

*I beseech you therefore, brethren, by the mercies of God, that ye present your bodies a living sacrifice, holy, acceptable unto God, which is your reasonable service. 2 And be not conformed to this world; but be ye transformed by the renewing of your mind, that ye may prove what is that good, and acceptable, and perfect will of God.*

Philippians 4:8

*Finally, brethren, whatsoever things are true, whatsoever things are honest, whatsoever things are just, whatsoever things are pure, whatsoever things are lovely, whatsoever things are of good report; if there be any virtue, and if there be any praise, think on these things.*

Colossians 3:16

*Let the word of Christ dwell in you richly in all wisdom; teaching and admonishing one another in psalms and hymns and spiritual songs, singing with grace in your hearts to the Lord.*

Though God does not speak specifically of listening here, it is implied. Without listening, there can be no effective teaching and admonishing. Also Ephesians 5:19, 20; Hebrews 3:12, 13.

1 Peter 2:1, 2

We are to lay aside certain activities and fill our minds with that which will bring spiritual growth. *1 Wherefore laying aside all malice, and all guile, and hypocrisies, and envies, and all evil speaking, 2 As newborn babes, desire the sincere milk of the word, that ye may grow thereby.*

2 Peter 1:3-9

In these verses we are reminded of our responsibility to mature in the Christian life, adding various characteristics which are listed. God has already made provision for them (v. 3); they become real in our lives as we appropriate the "exceeding great and precious promises" (v. 4). As we grow, we become fruitful for God (v. 8). The responsibility is ours.

1 John 2:15-17

*Love not the world, neither the things that are in the world. If any man love the world, the love of the Father is not in him. 16 For all that is in the world, the lust of the flesh, and the lust of the eyes, and the pride of life, is not of the Father, but is of the world. 17 And the world passeth away, and the lust thereof: but he that doeth the will of God abideth for ever.*

## 18. The almighty, eternal God of the universe, listens to man, his creation - incredible but true!

Psalm 34:4-6

David's testimony: *4 I sought the Lord, and he heard me, and delivered me from all my fears . . . . 6 This poor man cried, and the Lord heard him and saved him out of all his troubles.*

40:1

David again: *I waited patiently for the Lord; and he inclined unto me and heard my cry.*

77:1

*I cried unto the Lord with my voice, even unto God with my voice; and he gave ear unto me. Also 116:1, 2.*

94:9

*He that planteth the ear, shall he not hear? . . .*

Isaiah 59:1

*Behold the Lord's hand is not shortened, that it cannot save; neither his ear heaven, that it cannot hear.*

Jeremiah 29:12

God speaking through Jeremiah to the Jews held captive in Babylon: *12 Then shall ye call upon me and ye shall go and pray unto me, and I will hearken unto you.*

33:2, 3

God speaking to Jeremiah: *2 Thus saith the Lord the*

maker thereof, the Lord that formed it, to establish it: the Lord is his name; 3 Call unto me, and I will answer thee and shew thee great and mighty things which thou knowest not.

Ezekiel 35:12, 13

God's listening is not limited to our prayers: *12 And thou shalt know that I am the Lord, and that I have heard all thy blasphemies which thou hast spoken against the mountains of Israel . . . 13 Thus with your mouth ye have boasted against me: I have heard them.*

Matthew 21:22

Jesus speaking: *22 And all things whatsoever ye shall ask in prayer, believing, ye shall receive.*

Philippians 4:6, 7

*6 Be careful [anxious] for nothing; but in everything by prayer and thanksgiving let your requests be made known unto God. 7 And the peace of God, which passeth all understanding, shall keep your hearts and minds through Christ Jesus.*

James 4:2

*. . . Ye have not because ye ask not. Also James 5:16-18.*

## 19. As God listens to us, we should listen to others.

Exodus 12:26, 27

In his instructions for keeping the yearly Passover, God said parents were to listen to their children's questions: *26 . . . When your children shall say unto you, What mean ye by this service? 27 That ye shall say . . . .*

Joshua 4:6, 7

God directed Joshua to set up a memorial to the crossing of the Jordan river at flood season, and said similarly: *6 That this may be a sign among you, that when your children ask their fathers in time to come, saying, What mean ye by these stone? 7 Then ye shall answer them . . . .*

Job 29:11-13

The example of Job.

John 3:1-16

Jesus listened to the questions of Nicodemus, not ignoring them as we sometimes would.

6:5-11

Though Jesus knew what He intended to do to feed the five thousand, He listened to Philip and Andrew and made use of the boy's lunch, which was offered.

Proverbs 21:13

*Whoso stoppeth his ears at the cry of the poor, he also shall cry himself, but shall not be heard.*

# 7

## *Foreign Languages*

## CONCEPT SUMMARY

1. God originated languages.
2. The existence of a number of languages on the earth has a beneficial effect in the world of sin; it restrains men from uniting against God.
3. God has control over men's ability to speak and understand other languages.
4. Obedience to the commands of the Lord require going to people of all languages.
5. Learning to speak a language well depends on hearing it spoken consistently.
6. Language aptitude and/or experience can contribute to our usefulness in God's service.
7. Speaking in another language in public (or at least in a Christian meeting) is forbidden unless an interpreter is present to make the message meaningful.
8. Ability to speak in the languages of men, or even of angels, without love shown in attitude and actions counts for little.
9. In the Kingdom Age, after the judgment of the nations, the confusion of languages will end, and all will speak one language.
10. In Heaven all nations and languages will be represented.

**SCRIPTURAL BACKGROUND**

### 1. God originated languages.

Genesis 11:1-9

The Tower of Babel.*6 And the Lord said, Behold, the people is one, and they have all one language . . . 7 . . . let us go down, and there confound their language, that* they may not understand one another's speech . . . 9 . . . the Lord did there confound the language of all the earth: and from thence did the Lord scatter them abroad upon the face of all the earth.*

### 2. The existence of a number of languages has beneficial results in a world of sin; it restrains men from uniting against God.

Genesis 11:1-9

*1 And the whole earth was of one language and of one speech . . . 4 And they said, . . . let us build us a city and a tower, whose top may reach unto heaven; and let us make us a name lest we be scattered abroad upon the face of the whole earth . . . 6 And the Lord said, Behold the people is one and they have all one language; and this they begin to do; and now nothing will be restrained from them, which they have imagined to do. 7 Go to, let us go down, and there confound their language, that they may not understand one another's speech. 8 So the Lord scattered them abroad from thence upon the face of all the earth: and they left off to build a city.*

10:1-31

In describing the scattering of the population over many generations after the Flood, God records that they were divided by languages.

*1 Now these are the generations of the sons of Noah, Shem, Ham, and Japheth . . . . 2 The sons of Japheth . . . 5 By these were the isles of the Gentiles divided in their lands; every one after his tongue, after their families, in their nations. 20 These are the sons of Ham, after their families, after their tongues, in their countries, and in their nations. 31 These are the sons of Shem, after their families, after their tongues, in their lands, after their nations.*

## 3. God has control over men's ability to speak and understand other languages.

Genesis 11:1-9

God's purpose was that after the flood, men should be fruitful and multiply, and bring forth abundantly in the earth (Genesis 9:7). When men refused, it was He who broke down their ability to speak so that they understood one another.

Zephaniah 3:9

In the Kingdom Age, God will reverse the process: *9 For then will I turn to the people a pure language, that they may all call upon the name of the Lord, to serve him with one consent.*

Mark 16:15-17

Christ speaking to the eleven before His ascension: *15 . . . Go ye into all the world, and preach the gospel to every creature . . . . 17 And these signs shall follow them that believe . . . they shall speak with other tongues.*

Acts 2:5-12

People of many languages each heard in his own language on the Day of Pentecost, as the Holy Spirit worked.

*6 . . . The multitude came together, and were confounded, because that every man heard them speak in his own language. 7 And they were all amazed and marvelled, saying one to another, Behold, are not all these which speak Galileans? 8 And how hear we every man in our own tongue, wherein we were born? [Verses 9-11 list sixteen geographical areas represented.] 11 . . . We do hear them speak in our tongues the wonderful works of God. 12 And they were all amazed, and were in doubt, saying one to another, What meaneth this?*

10:46 and 11:15-18

Peter preached Christ to the people assembled at the house of Cornelius, a Gentile (v. 34-43); the Holy Spirit came upon those who believed; as a result, those who had come with Peter were astonished. Why? *46 For they heard them speak with tongues and glorify God.*

Later Peter, in answering the criticism of the Jewish Christians in Jerusalem for his going to the Gentiles, said:

*15 And as I began to speak, the Holy Ghost fell on them, as on us at the beginning. 16 Then remembered I the word of the Lord, how that he said, . . . Ye shall be baptized with the Holy Spirit. 17 Forasmuch then as God gave them the like gift as he did unto us, who believed on the Lord Jesus Christ; what was I that I could withstand God? 18 When they heard these things they held their peace, and glorified God . . . .*

19:5, 6

At Ephesus Paul spoke with a group of twelve disciples of John the Baptist, preaching Christ. *5 When they heard this, they were baptized in the name of the Lord Jesus. 6 And when Paul laid his hands upon them, the Holy Ghost came on them; and they spake with tongues, and prophesied.*

1 Corinthians 12:4-31

*4 Now there are diversities of gifts, but the same Spirit. 5 And there are differences of administrations, but the same Lord. 7 But the manifestation of the Spirit is given to every man to profit withal. 8 For to one is given by the Spirit the word of wisdom . . . to another divers kinds of tongues; to another the interpretation of tongues: 11 But all these worketh that one and self-same Spirit, dividing to every man severally as he will.* Also verses 28-30.

## 4. Obedience to the commands of the Lord requires going to people of all languages.

Matthew 28:19, 20

*19 Go ye therefore, and teach all nations, baptizing . . . 20 Teaching them to observe all things whatsoever I have commanded you . . . .*

Mark 16:15

*Go ye into all the world, and preach the gospel to every creature.*

Acts 1:8

*. . . Ye shall be witnesses unto me both in Jerusalem, and in all Judea, and in Samaria, and unto the uttermost part of the earth.*

Romans 14:11, 12

No matter what language people speak, they are accountable to God. *11 . . . Every knee shall bow to me, and every tongue shall confess to God. 12 So then every one of us shall give account of himself to God.*

Also Revelation 20:12, 13 - "every man", in verse 13.

## 5. Learning to speak a language well depends on hearing it spoken consistently.

Nehemiah 13:23-27

An interesting example in the testimony of Nehemiah: *23 In those days also saw I Jews that had married wives of Ashdod, of Ammon, and of Moab: 24 And their children spake half in the speech of Ashdod, and could not speak the Jews' language, but according to the language of each people. 25 And I contended with them . . . .*

The real condemnation here is for intermarriage to heathen partners, but one result was the lack of facility in the children's use of their fathers' language.

## 6. Language aptitude and/or experience can contribute to our usefulness in God's service.

Daniel 1:3, 4

Daniel and his friends were chosen by a pagan king, Nebuchadnezzar, and greatly used by God because of their ability. *3 And the king spake unto . . . the master of his eunuchs that he should bring certain of the children of Israel . . . 4 Children in whom was no blemish . . . skilful in all wisdom, and cunning in knowledge, and understanding science, and such as had ability in them to stand in the king's palace, and whom they might teach the learning and the tongue of the Chaldeans.*

Acts 7:22

*And Moses was learned in all the wisdom of the Egyptians, and was mighty in words and in deeds.*

Though we are nowhere told specifically that Joseph spoke the Egyptian language, it is evident that he did, or he doubtless would not have been given such high position in Egypt; also the fact that his brothers did not recognize him points in this direction.

## 7. Speaking in another language in public, or at least in a Christian meeting, is forbidden unless an interpreter is present to make the message meaningful.

1 Corinthians 14:2-28

*9 . . . Except ye utter by the tongue words easy to be understood, how shall it be known what is spoken? for ye shall speak into the air . . . 13 Wherefore let him that speaketh in an unknown tongue pray that he may interpret . . . 16 Else when thou shalt bless with the spirit, how shall he that occupieth the room of the unlearned say Amen at thy giving of thanks, seeing he understandeth not what thou sayest: . . . 28 . . . If there be no interpreter, let him keep silence in the church; and let him speak to himself and to God.*

## 8. Ability to speak in the languages of man, or even of angels, without love shown in attitude and actions counts for little.

1 Corinthians 13

*1 Though I speak with the tongues of men and of angels, and have not charity, I am become as sounding brass, or a tinkling cymbal.*

*4 Charity suffereth long, and is kind; charity envieth not; charity vaunteth not itself, is not puffed up, 5 Doth not behave itself unseemly, seeketh not her own, is not easily provoked, thinketh no evil; 6 Rejoiceth not in iniquity, but rejoiceth in the truth; 7 Beareth all things, believeth all things, hopeth all things, endureth all things.*

*8 Charity never faileth: but whether there be prophecies, they shall fail; whether there be tongues, they shall cease; whether there be knowledge, it shall vanish away.*

## 9. In the Kingdom Age, after the judgment of the nations, the confusion of languages will end, and all will speak one language.

Zephaniah 3:9

*For then will I turn to the people a pure language, that they may all call upon the name of the Lord, to serve him with one consent.*

(NASB) *For then will I give to the people purified lips, That all of them may call on the name of the Lord, To serve Him shoulder to shoulder.*

H. A. Ironside: "Then shall the confusion of Babel be undone, and the Lord will give to all peoples a pure language . . . ." *Notes on the Minor Prophets* (N.Y.: Loizeaux, 1947) p. 316.

Norman Jerome: "After the day of judgment, there will be only one language: all will speak the language of God."

"Israel's Future Glory," in *Bible Knowledge*, July, August, September, 1957 (Wheaton, IL: Scripture Press) p. 591.

## 10. In Heaven all nations and languages will be represented.

Revelation 5:9

Worship to the Lamb is expressed thus: *9 . . . Thou art worthy . . . for thou wast slain, and hast redeemed us to God by thy blood out of every kindred, and tongue, and people, and nation.*

7:9

*And this I beheld, and lo, a great multitude, which no man could number, of all nations, and kindreds, and people, and tongues, stood before the throne, and before the Lamb, clothed with white robes . . . .*

### LANGUAGES: HOW IMPORTANT?

Charles V used to say that "the more languages a man knew, he was so many times more a man." Each new form of human speech introduces one into a new world of thought and life.   -- Roger Ascham
1515-1568

A man who is ignorant of foreign languages is ignorant of his own.   -- Johann Goethe
1749-1832

To acquire a few tongues is the task of a few years; to be eloquent in one is the labor of a life.

-- Charles Haddon Spurgeon
1834-1892

Every language is a temple in which the soul of those who speak it is enshrined. -- Oliver Wendell Holmes
1809-1894

# *Resources*

## STUDY MATERIALS FOR THE TEACHER

The following list of resources has been compiled from several sources and represents varied viewpoints. They are not sources from which this volume has been produced, but rather materials which teachers may find helpful in implementing a Christian viewpoint in the classroom. All have been recommended by someone in the Christian school field.

### BOOKS

Ackerman, Carl. *The Bible in Shakespeare.* Norwood, PA: Norwood Editions, 1977. 124 p. Deals with Shakespeare's knowledge of the Bible, his use of Bible language, Biblical history and persons, religious and moral principles. Very helpful.

Baron, Henry J. *Dirty Books in Christian Schools: Principles of Selection.* Grand Rapids: Christian Schools International, 1970. 32 p. An examination of the "place of controversial literature in the school's curriculum from the points of view of the writer, student, teacher, and parent."

Bartel, Roland, ed. *Biblical Images in Literature.* Nashville: Abingdon Press, 1975. 432 p. "Forty-one articles analyze the works of well-known writers which stress the use of biblical allusion." Three sections: poetry, drama, fiction.

Batson, Beatrice. *A Reader's Guide to Religious Literature.* Chicago: Moody Press, 1968. 188 p. A survey of Christian classics since Dante, arranged by historical periods. Includes detailed description of each work, concise biography of its author. Major emphasis on writers before 20th Century.

Berg, Viola. *Pathways for the Poet.* Milford, MI: Mott Media, 1977. A resource book for poetry teachers and students. Defines and gives examples of 200 poetry forms. Includes classroom techniques.

Beveridge, Albert J. *The Bible as Good Reading.* Philadelphia: Henry Altemus, 1907. 94 p. Beveridge was a U. S. Senator from Indiana. He shows how reading the Bible as "an account of mighty men and extraordinary women is fascinating and leads to seeing the Bible as religion."

Chase, Mary Ellen. *The Bible and the Common Reader.* N. Y.: Macmillan, 1952. 381 p. Though this author does not accept the authority of the Bible, or verbal plenary inspiration, she shows much in her beginning chapters of the significance of the Bible, with many examples of Biblical expressions in everyday speech.

Frye, Roland M. *Shakespeare and Christian Doctrine.* Princeton, NJ: Princeton University Press, 1963. 314 p. The purpose of the book is to "consider the relation between Shakespearean drama and Christian theology."

Fulghum, W. B., Jr. *A Dictionary of Biblical Allusions in English Literature.* N. Y.: Holt, Rinehart and Winston, 1965. 291 p. Designed to help the reader locate an allusion in the Bible itself and to understand its meaning and use in literature.

Fuller, Edmund. *Books with Men behind Them.* N.Y.: Random House, 1962. 241 p. Concerned with the image of man portrayed in contemporary writing, Fuller explores that "image in the work of a number of writers of widely differing characteristics, who have in common . . . a mature vision of man."

Fuller, Edmund. *Man in Modern Fiction.* N. Y.: Random House, 1958. 171 p. "Appraises the validity and implications of the image of man from a perspective found in the Judeo-Christian tradition." Shows the distortion in modern writing. A companion book to *Books with Men behind Them*, which is more positive.

Graef, Hilda. *Modern Gloom and Christian Hope.* Chicago: Henry Regnery Co., 1959. 143 p. A criticism of the contemporary literary scene from the Catholic point of view. A challenge to existentialism. Fully documented.

Gros, Louis, and others. *Literary Interpretations of Biblical Narratives.* Nashville: Abingdon Press, 1974. 352 p. Contains the substance of the five years of institutes at Indiana University on Teaching the Bible in Secondary English. Applies the tools of literary criticism to aid the teacher in preparing a course in the Bible as literature.

Howard, Thomas. *Antique Drum: The World as Image.* Phila.: J. B. Lippincott, 1969. 157 p. Shows how man's actions and literature are unconsciously based on the idea that the world does make sense - a view not generally accepted by humanistic writers. Written by a teacher of English.

Hunt, Gladys. *Honey for a Child's Heart.* Grand Rapids: Zondervan Publishing House, 1969. Revised, 1978. 182 p. Designed to help parents stimulate an interest in choosing and reading good books. Includes 50 pages of annotated bibliography, listing books for wholesome reading, some of which are specifically Christian.

Jellema, Roderick, ed. *Contemporary Writers in Christian Perspective*. Grand Rapids: Eerdmans, 1967. A series of 48-page booklets, each on a specific literary work.

Kepler, Thomas, compiler. *An Anthology of Devotional Literature*. Grand Rapids: Baker Book House, 1977. A collection of devotional thoughts from various backgrounds and cultures over 18 centuries. Christian.

Kilby, Clyde S. *The Christian World of C. S. Lewis*. Grand Rapids: Eerdmans, 1964. 216 p. An introduction to Lewis's Christian writings and to the shaping influences in his life.

Killinger, John. *The Failure of Theology in Modern Literature*. Nashville: Abingdon, 1963. 239 p. Though not written from an evangelical viewpoint, helpful in understanding modern literature.

Koopman, Leroy. *Beauty Care for the Tongue*. Grand Rapids: Zondervan, 1972. 100 p. A study of Biblical teaching concerning the use of the tongue, with suggestions for group study. Uses RSV primarily.

Lamar, Nedra Newkirk. *How to Speak the Written Word*. Old Tappan, NJ: Fleming H. Revell. 192 p. A "guide to natural, conversational reading of the printed word . . . without resorting to personal interpretation." A special section on how to read the Bible.

Lee, Charlotte I. *Oral Reading of the Scriptures*. Atlanta: Houghton, Mifflin, 1974. 198 p. Includes many suggestions for the teacher who teaches oral reading and speech and wishes to include Scripture portions. Relatively free from theological controversy. Accepts the Bible as is; places the emphasis on the reading of it.

Lewis, C. S. *The Discarded Image*. N. Y.: Cambridge University Press, 1968. On medieval and Renaissance literature.

Lewis, C. S., ed. *Essays Presented to Charles Williams*. Grand Rapids: Eerdmans, 1966. 145 p. A collection of essays on literary topics, written by Dorothy Sayers, J. R. R. Tolkien, C. S. Lewis, A. O. Barfield, Gervase Matthews, and W. H. Lewis.

Lewis, C. S. *The Literary Impact of the Authorized Version*. Philadelphia: Fortress Press, 1963. 37 p.

Lewis, C. S. *A Preface to "Paradise Lost."* London: Oxford University Press, 1967 (First published in 1942). 143 p. An analysis and commentary on Milton's *Paradise Lost*, by a believer whose lifetime study was in the field of medieval and Renaissance literature.

Lindskoog, Kathryn and John. *How to Grow a Young Reader*. Elgin, IL: David C. Cook Publishing Co. 168 p. Written for parents, but includes much help for teachers, and a "shopper's guide to more than 400 good books available to children today, from the classics to brand-new titles."

Lockerbie, D. Bruce. *The Liberating Word*. Grand Rapids: Eerdmans, 1974. 124 p. "Explores the concept of creativity from a Christian prespective. Deals with myth and its relation to art, creative imagination and the Gospel."

Martin, David. *Teaching English*. Crockett, KY: Rod and Staff Publishers. 24 p. Reprinted from *Christian School Builder*, as an aid to English teachers in Christian schools.

Meeter, Merle, and Stanley Wiersma. *Contrasting Approaches to Teaching Literature*. Grand Rapids: Calvin College Monograph, 1970.

Noble, Richmond. *Shakespeare's Biblical Knowledge and Use of the Book of Common Prayer*. London: S.P.C.K., 1935.

Ryken, Leland. *The Literature of the Bible*. Grand Rapids: Zondervan Publishing House, 1974. 356 p. A fascinating book growing out of a Wheaton College course in Biblical literature. Written from a literary viewpoint but based on a recognition of the Bible as God's Word to man. An excellent resource.

Slater, Rosalie J. *The Christian History Literature Series*. I. *Children and Literature in the American Christian School;* II. *The Christian Literature of the American Revolution*. San Francisco: Foundation for American Christian Education. In preparation as of February, 1980. "The impact of the westward movement of Christianity on literature."

Stewart, Randall. *American Literature and Christian Doctrine*. Baton Rouge: Louisiana State University Press, 1958. 154 p.

Thomas, I. D. E., ed. *The Golden Treasury of Puritan Quotations*. Chicago: Moody Press, 1975. 350 p. Over 1500 quotations arranged under more than one hundred topical headings. Acquaints students with our rich heritage from great Puritans.

Webster, Noah. *The American Dictionary of the English Language.* San Francisco: Foundation for American Christian Education. 2000 p. "The first and only American Christian dictionary. Word definitions are, in the main, based on Biblical usage and meaning of words." A facsimile of the 1828 edition. Includes essay, *Noah Webster: Founding Father of American Scholarship and Education,* by Rosalie Slater.

Yoder, Sanford Calvin. *Poetry of the Old Testament.* Scottdale, PA: Herald Press, 1952. 426 p. A classic from a warm evangelical who accepts the entire Bible as inspired and authoritative. Includes chapters on Hebrew culture and history as a background for the poetry. "Acquaints students with great scriptural truths through poetry. Includes all poetic portions of Pentateuch and Historical Books, plus the Books of Poetry. Follows KJ Version.

Zylstra, Henry. *Testament of Vision.* Grand Rapids: Eerdmans, 1965. 144 p. Explores the values of teaching and studying literature in order to understand life. By a long-time college teacher of literature.

## CASSETTE TAPES

Each year a number of Christian school associations make available tapes of workshops which are part of their teachers' conventions. Some of these present specific programs; some give hints and practical suggestions for the classroom; others deal with teaching a specifically Christian viewpoint.

Illustrative of what is available on a continuing basis is the following list of language arts and English tapes from the last several years' conventions of the Mid-Atlantic Christian School Association. The source of these tapes is Heritage Gospel Productions, Inc., R. D. 1, Stevens, PA 17578. You may wish to write for their MACSA Tape Catalog.

| | |
|---|---|
| Barker, Nicholas. | *How Unimportant for the Christian Are Literature and Fine Arts?* |
| | *How Do We Know Literature?* |
| Baxter, Harold. | *Who Needs Modern Fiction?* |
| Chappell, Dwight | *Readability of the Bible (two tapes)* |
| Clawson, Penny | *Aslan, the Lion and the Lamb* |
| Daugherty, James | *The Gifted Child and Speed Reading* |
| Ewbank, Frances W. | *Fact, Fiction, Fantasy and Faith: Imaginative Literature and Its Contribution to the Christian Life* |
| Fink, Carol | *Johnny Can Write and Enjoy Writing* |
| | *Learning and Using Grammatical Principles* |
| Gaskins, Irene | *Teaching Language Arts to Poor Learners* |
| | *How to Teach Reading Skills Five Hours a Day* |
| | *Reading Methods and Materials: How to Choose* |
| | *Phonics and Spelling* |
| | *How to Teach Sight Words* |
| Hershberger, Myrna | *Units in the Foreign Language* |
| Hunt, Gladys | *Children and Literature* |
| | *Adolescents and Literature* |
| | *Creative Writing* |
| Lake, Larry | *Writing a Book Review* |
| Miller, John | *The Integration of the Bible and Literature* |
| Rand, Phyllis | *Creative Writing for Upper Elementary* |
| | *Using the Classics to Teach Reading* |
| Schimmer, Jane | *The Dyslexic Child* |
| Shaida, Pete | *Remediation of Speech and Language Problems* |
| Showalter, Louise | *A Mock Trip to Mexico - Teach Culture and Encourage Speaking* |
| Sonnekalb, Christine | *Pros and Cons of Foreign Language in Junior High* |
| Stong, Jean | *Dysgraphia: Parts I and II (two tapes)* |
| Taylor, Dora | *Motivating the Foreign Language Student* |
| Tress, Gretchen | *Beginning Reading: What Is It All About?* |
| Wyand, Becky | *Champions in Reading - How? (Victory Drill Book presentation)* |
| | *Research for Young Students* |
| Yoder, Keith | *Moral Development and the New Realism in Children's Literature* |

Another source is the Association of Christian Schools International, which with Grace College sponsors the National Institute of Christian School Administration and the National Institute of Christian School Teachers each summer at Winona Lake, Indiana. They also make tapes available after the institutes. Send for their list and prices. The address: ACSI, 464 Malin Road, Newtown Square, PA  19073.

## CURRICULUM MATERIALS

Since publishers' addresses are listed in the Directory which follows this listing, only abbreviated designations are given here.

### READING

*Basic Bible Readers* (Standard Publishing)
  Five books, Primer - Grade 4, with controlled vocabulary. Selected Bible stories, poetry, and prayers children can read for themselves.

Beka *Beginning Reading Program* (A Beka Books)
  Series designed for K and advanced K, including basic phonics series, *Little Books*, *Little Owl Books*, and *Big Owl Books*.

Beka *Phonics and Numbers Workbooks* (A Beka Books)
  A series of nine workbooks for young children, N-3.

*Beka Supplementary Readers* (A Beka Books)
  Four books: *Primary Bible Reader* (K-3), *Aesop's Fables for Young Readers* (1-2), *All Kinds of Animals* (2-3), *Pilgrim's Progress Simplified* (3-4), with teacher's manual.

*The Bible Nurture and Reader Series* (Rod and Staff)
  Grades 1-4. A comprehensive series including reading, phonics, English, writing and spelling. Uses Bible stories. Readers, workbooks, teacher's manuals, flashcards, etc. Illustrations are conservative Mennonite.

*The Character Builders* (Christian School Curriculum)
  A series of 24 books designed for three groups: Grades K-2, 3-5, and 6-8. Each book teaches three Christian traits, using Bible and modern stories. Not designed to teach reading, but valuable as supplementary material. 1980.

*The Christian Reading Series* (A Beka Books)
  A series of ten readers for Grades 1-3, with grade level teacher's manuals.

*Developing Better Reading* (Rod and Staff)
  Grade 2 to adults. For poor readers. Designed for a six to eight week concentrated study in phonics and comprehension. Pupil's workbook, teacher's manual, flash cards.

*God Is Good Series* (Rod and Staff)
  A set of seven books designed to give reading practice to pupils using the *Bible Nurture and Reading Series*.

*Green Lights Phonics* (Christian Light)
  Grade 1. A six weeks course in phonics for pre-readers in Grade 1. Prepared originally for children of Pennsylvania Dutch background. Pupil's book, teacher's manual, chart.

*I Can Read a Bible Story Series* (Concordia)
  A series of six readers for children.  1976.

*Learning to Read from the Bible Primers* (Zondervan)
  A series of four books for pre-school and Grade 1.

*Learning to Read from the Bible Readers* (Zondervan)
  A series of four Bible readers based on a programmed vocabulary. Grades 1-3. 1976.

McGuffey's *Eclectic Readers* (Lynn Publishers)

A series of seven books, printed as facsimiles of the nineteenth century series which were so widely used. Workbooks available for Primer, Books 1 and 2, from Fairfax Christian Bookstore.

*Modern McGuffey Readers: The Golden Rule Series* (A Beka Books)

Modern stories and retelling of classics. Emphasis on basic principles for successful living. Readers at five levels, teacher's manuals. Reprinted for Christian schools.

*Of America Reading Series* (A Beka Books)

Series of four books for grades 4-6. Character-building, patriotic.

*Pathway Readers* (Rod and Staff)

A series of three books for Grades 6, 7, 8, especially for Amish Christian schools. Published in Canada, but available from Rod and Staff.

*A Phonics Manual for Teachers* (A Beka Books)

A phonics program for an entire year. Includes material from the first and second grade curriculum guides. Other related phonics aids available.

*Poetry Guide, K-6* (Christian Schools International)

Includes source index, out-of-print poems, suggestions for integration across grade levels and subjects. 59 p. 1970.

*Programmed Reading from the Scriptures* (Programmed Reading)

A series of 17 paperback programmed books, covering Genesis 1-37, developing a reading vocabulary of over 1000 words. Developed especially for use with inner city children and youth who need help in learning to read. By a former missionary and teacher of first grade and LD children. Books 1-7 in preparation; Books 8-17 available. 1978.

*Reading for Fun and Enrichment* (A Beka Books)

Fifty-five small books designed for summer reading by children who have been in the Beka kindergarten program. Suitable for other purposes as well. 1979.

*Self Pronouncing Alphabet Pre-Kindergarten and Beginning to Read Programs* (Beacon)

A comprehensive program for beginning readers, including readers, drill materials, work books, filmstrips, teacher training materials, etc.

*Victory Drill Reading Program* (Heritage Academy)

A phonics-based program designed to develop rapid word recognition, accurate pronunciation and spelling. Student book, teacher's manual, reproducible worksheets, cassette.


**LANGUAGE ARTS** (other than reading)


Beka *Language* (A Beka Books)
Workbooks and test booklets for Grades 2-6.

Beka *Grammar and Composition* (A Beka Books)
Workbooks and test booklets for Grades 7-12.

*The Building Christian English Series* (Rod and Staff)
Grades 3-7. Pupil's texts, teacher's manuals, unit test booklets. Also supplementary English worksheets are available and may be used with the above series or separately.

*Creative Writing Ideas - Early Impressions* (Association of Christian Schools International) A packet of activity cards for early childhood.

*Creative Writing Starters - Lunch Box* (Association of Christian Schools International) A box of 150 cards, each giving a starting idea for writing a paragraph or a story. Designed to stimulate thinking; based on the five senses.

*Cursive Writing Simplified* (A Beka Books)

A teacher's manual with practice sentences which include character quotations and Bible verses.

*Easy English*, by Dick Bohrer (Multnomah)

A supplementary workbook for Grades 7-12. Teaches grammar, using literature and a football theme. Includes exams, study sheets, answer pages. 1978.

*Language and Man*, by Dan Vander Ark and Bruce Hekman (Christian Schools International) A nine-week unit exploring what language means, how it grows, how it affects people. 36 p. 1974.

*Language Arts Curriculum Guide, K-6*, by Nelle Vander Ark (Christian Schools International) Includes primary and intermediate programs, creative dramatics, literary heritage list. 116 p. 1967.

*Lifepacs* in Language Arts (Alpha Omega)

A sequential series of modules for use in English, elementary and secondary. May be used in traditional or individualized classroom, and purchased according to need. 1978.

Also, a modification of the Alpha Omega curriculum is available especially for Mennonite schools. It is entitled *Christian Light Education*, from Christian Light Publications. 1979.

*Personalized Educational Progress in Grammar*, by Pam Luinberg (Christian Schools International) A series of ten personalized modules on grammar, enabling students to learn at their own paces. Includes student modules, worksheets and tests, teacher's manual, cassettes. Available only in trial edition as of February, 1980. Grades 6-12

*Spelling and Poetry* (A Beka Books)

Weekly word lists for grades 1-12, along with poetry to be memorized at each grade level. Instructions for the teacher, correlated poetry tapes for grades 4-6.

*Spelling by Sound and Structure* (Rod and Staff)

Grade 4. Weekly lessons for the year, including Bible words, stories and characters. Phonics approach. Pupil's book and answer key.

*Spelling Spectra*, by Sheri Haan and Joy Witte (Christian Schools International) A complete basic spelling series from a Christian perspective. Levels 2-6. In trial stage as of February, 1980.

*Write the Word*, by William Folprecht (Mott Media)

An illustrated creative writing text for Christian high school students. Practical suggestions for beginning authors; includes advice on selling your manuscript. 224 p. 1976.

*A Writing Program, Grades 7-12*, by Nelle Vander Ark and Bruce Hekman

(Christian Schools International) A resource book and guide for teaching composition sequentially. 124 p. 1968.

*Writing with Phonics* (A Beka Books)

A four book series for K4, K5, and Grades 1 and 2. Includes phonics, manuscript and cursive writing.


## LITERATURE

*Aspects of English Series* (Holt, Rinehart and Winston)

A series of eleven books, each including selected writings from one author or type of literature, along with discussion questions. Edited by D. Bruce Lockerbie, and in several cases prepared by him. While not specifically Christian in viewpoint, they reflect the wholesome views of the Christian editor.

Beka *Literature Series* (A Beka Books)

Three volumes for Grades 7, 8, 9: *Of People; Of Places; Of Ideas*. The emphases in the three books are character, settings, and themes.

*Literature 4, 5, 6*, for Grades 10-12, scheduled for completion in 1980. Include traditional and modern stories, essays, plays and poems of high literary quality. Christian in content and interpretation.

*Christian Literature Supplement* (Christian Light)

A compilation of stories and poems selected for Christian high school literature.

*Country of the Risen King*, by Merle Meeter, compiler (Baker Book House)

"An anthology of 120 Christian poets, all followers of Christ, whose poems grow out of their Christian experience." Scripture used as a basis for evaluation, along with study of artistry, and other literary characteristics. 1978.

*Lifeview: A Christian Approach to Literature Studies* (Mott Media)

Teacher and student guides for use in high school or Bible college literature courses. Includes analyses, commentaries, workbooks on novels most frequently studied. Guides available for 13 books; more in preparation.

*Literature for Christian Schools Series* (Bob Jones University Press)

*American Literature for Christian Schools; English Literature for Christian Schools.* In each case, a collection of appropriate literature, together with historical and biographical background and a Christian view.

*Literature of the Bible Series* (Literature of the Bible)

A series of six illustrated student manuals, with accompanying teacher's guides. Edited by Leland Ryken. Designed for school use in teaching the Bible, or portions of it, as literature. Uses RSV Bible in the student books. Some art may be questionable in Christian schools. Teacher's guides may be used independently however, with students using their own Bibles as texts. 1976.

*Man and the Outcast; Man and the Search for Self; Man and the Search for Spiritual Significance.* By Dan Vander Ark and others. (Christian Schools International) Three literature units for senior high based on the individual reading approach in which students read on their own and keep a journal of their responses. 1971, 1974.

*Pilgrim's Progress Study Guides* (Christian Light)

Separate guides for Part I and Part II.

*Pilot Series in Literature*, by Beth Merizon and others (National Union of Christian Schools and Eerdmans) Books I, II, III, for Grades 7-9. 1957-1964.

*Purposeful Writing*, by D. Bruce Lockerbie (Addison-Wesley)

Applies the principles of speech-making to writing. A clear approach to creative writing for high school and college students. Text edition and teacher's guide. 1972. Grades 11, 12.

*Soundings Series*, edited by Henry Baron and others (Christian Schools International) A series of five literature books for Grades 6-9. Designed to encourage readers to explore themselves and their relationships on the basis of their primary relationship to God. 1976.

*Teaching Literature Thematically, 10-12*, by Nelle Vander Ark and Henry J. Baron (Christian Schools International) "Insights into familiar selections based on the theme: Humans Pursued and Pursuing." 63 p. 1967.

*Thematic Literature Units*, by Henry Baron, editor (National Union of Christian Schools) A thematic approach to teaching the *Pilot Series*, supplemented by other resources. Twelve units, four for each grade, with Christian perspective. 1970.

*Thematic Teaching Units, Grade 10* (Christian Schools International)

By Bruce Hekman. Two units on themes: Survival, and Man in Society. 51 p. 1968.

*Touchstone Series*, edited by Henry Baron and others (National Union of Christian Schools) Grades 9, 10. Four anthologies, each based on a theme to be considered from a Christian perspective: *Around Us; Within Us; Between Us; Above Us.* 1973.

## BOOKLISTS

*Bible-Related Curriculum Materials*, edited by Thayer Warshaw. (Abingdon) 1976. 168 p.

*Books Worth Reading Aloud*, by Sheri Haan. (Christian Schools International)

1978. An annotated selection of good books, most of which are not specifically Christian, but wholesome.

*Honey for a Child's Heart*, by Gladys Hunt. (Zondervan) Revised, 1978.

Includes about fifty pages listing, with annotations, recommended books for children. Books are not specifically Christian, for the most part.

*How to Grow a Young Reader.* by Kathryn and John Lindskoog. (David C. Cook)

1980. 168 p. Includes a list of more than 400 good books for children, from the classics to the brand-new.

*Library Materials Guide.* (Christian Schools International)

Over 500 reviews by more than 100 reviewers to assist in book selection.

*Recommended Book List* (Christian Light)
A list of books recommended by Paradise Mennonite School, for Grades 1-10. Revised.

*Books for Small Children; Humane Literature for Young Readers; Books for the Middle Years of Schooling; Humane Literature in High Schools.* Four *Textbook Evaluation Reports*, by Russell Kirk. Though not written from an evangelical Christian viewpoint, these 8-page reports provide helpful annotated lists of conservative books. Free upon request.

## DIRECTORY OF PUBLISHERS

As far as possible current addresses of publishers are included below. A few companies whose publications are listed as resources are either no longer in business, or are not listed in *Books in Print*. Where a publisher has several addresses, an attempt has been made to provide the one to which orders should be sent.

Abingdon Press
201 Eighth Avenue South
Nashville, TN 37202

Addison-Wesley Publishing Co.
Jacob Way
Reading, MA 01867

Alpha Omega Publications
P. O. Box 3153
Tempe, AZ 85281

America's Future
542 Main Street
New Rochelle, NY 10801

Association of Christian Schools
    International (for books)
P. O. Box 4097
Whittier, CA 90607
    (for tapes)
464 Malin Road
Newtown Square, PA 19073

Baker Book House
P. O. Box 6287
Grand Rapids, MI 49506

Beacon Enterprises, Inc.
P. O. Box 1296
Santa Cruz, CA 95061

A Beka Books
Pensacola Christian College
125 St. John Street
Pensacola, FL 32503

Bob Jones University Press, Inc.
Greenville, SC 29614

Calvin College
Grand Rapids, MI 49506

Cambridge University Press
510 North Avenue
New Rochelle, NY 10801

Christian Light Publications
P. O. Box 1126
Harrisonburg, VA 22801

Christian School Curriculum
(A Division of Fleming H. Revell)
Old Tappan, NJ 07675

Christian Schools International
(formerly NUCS)
3350 E. Paris Avenue S. E.
Grand Rapids, MI 49508
    or
P. O. Box 39
Norwich, Ontario NOJ-1PO

Concordia Publishing House
3558 South Jefferson Avenue
St. Louis, MO 63118

Cook, David C., Publishing Co.
850 North Grove
Elgin, IL 60120

Eerdmans, William B., Publishing Co.
255 Jefferson Avenue S. E.
Grand Rapids, MI 49503

Fairfax Christian Bookstore
11121 Pope's Head Road
Fairfax, VA 22030

Fortress Press
2900 Queen Lane
Philadelphia, PA 19129

Foundation for American Christian
    Education
2946 25th Avenue
San Francisco, CA 94132

Herald Press
616 Walnut Avenue
Scottdale, PA 15683

Heritage Academy, Inc.
Route 2, Box 264
Hagerstown, MD 21740

Heritage Gospel Productions, Inc.
R. D. 1
Stevens, PA 17578

Holt, Rinehart and Winston, Inc.
383 Madison Avenue
New York, NY 10017

Houghton, Mifflin
Wayside Road
Burlington, MA 01803

Lippincott, J. B., Co.
521 Fifth Avenue
New York, NY 10017

Literature of the Bible, Inc.
P. O. Box 27067
Chicago, IL 60627
    or
P. O. Box 134
Downsview, Ontario M3M3A3

Louisiana State University Press
Baton Rouge, LA 70803

Lynn Publishers
P. O. Box 2024
Staunton, VA 24401

Macmillan Publishing Co., Inc.
Riverside, NJ 08075

Moody Press
1777 Shermer Road
Northbrook, IL 60062

Mott Media
305 Caroline
Milford, MI 48042

Multnomah Press
10209 S. E. Division Street
Portland, OR 97266

National Union of Christian Schools
(NUCS) See Christian Schools
International

Norwood Editions
P. O. Box 38
Norwood, PA 19074

Oxford University Press
16-00 Pollitt Drive
Fair Lawn, NJ 07410

Princeton University Press
41 William Street
Princeton, NJ 08540

Programmed Reading Publications
285 Hill Avenue
Glen Ellyn, IL 60137

Random House
127 East 59th Street, Room 201
New York, NY 10022

Revell, Fleming H., Co.
184 Central Avenue
Old Tappan, NJ 07675

Rod and Staff Publishers
Crockett, KY 41413

Standard Publishing Co.
8121 Hamilton Avenue
Cincinnati, OH 45231

Zondervan Publishing House
1415 Lake Drive S. E.
Grand Rapids, MI 49506

# *Index*

# About the Author ...

Dr. Ruth C. Haycock is a recognized leader in the field of Christian school education. She has served as a workshop leader for numerous Christian school conventions, and has been a consultant for the Association of Christian Schools International. She is an instructor each summer at the National Institute of Christian School Administration at Grace College and is a member of the Advisory Board for Christian School Curriculum, a Division of Fleming H. Revell, publishers.

Dr. Haycock currently serves as Chairman of Christian School Education at Piedmont Bible College in Winston-Salem, North Carolina. She is Professor Emeritus at Baptist Bible College of Pennsylvania where she taught for thirty-six years. She is a graduate of Baptist Bible Seminary and holds a Bachelors Degree from the University of Minnesota and both Masters and Doctorate in Education from Syracuse University.

Dr. Haycock is a member of *Pi Lambda Theta* and *Phi Beta Kappa.* She is listed in *Outstanding Educators in America, Who's Who in Religion*, and *International Who's Who in Education.* She has been a contributor to *An Introduction to Evangelical Christian Education, Church Educational Agencies, Adult Education in the Church*, and *Childhood Education in the Church.* She is a regular contributor to *Daybreak*, a bimonthly publication of Piedmont Bible College.